Mountains
of the Moon

There aren't two categories of people.

There aren't some that were born to have
        everything,
    leaving the rest with nothing,
and a majority that has nothing
    and cannot taste the happiness
that God has created for all.

The Christian society that God wants
    is one in which we share the goodness
that God has given for everyone.

                    Archbishop Oscar Romero

Mountains of the Moon

STORIES
ABOUT
SOCIAL
JUSTICE

EDITED BY
STEPHANIE WELLER HANSON

Saint Mary's Press
Christian Brothers Publications
Winona, Minnesota

Short Fiction Books from Saint Mary's Press

Waking Up Bees
STORIES OF LIVING LIFE'S QUESTIONS

Mountains of the Moon
STORIES ABOUT SOCIAL JUSTICE

 Genuine recycled paper with 10% post-consumer waste. Printed with soy-based ink.

The quotation on page 2 is from *The Violence of Love: The Pastoral Wisdom of Archbishop Oscar Romero,* compiled and translated by James R. Brockman (San Francisco: Harper and Row, 1988), page 212. Copyright © 1988 by the Chicago Province of the Society of Jesus.

The publishing team included Barbara Allaire, series editor; Stephanie Weller Hanson, development editor; Rebecca Fairbank, copy editor; Barbara Bartelson, production editor; Hollace Storkel, typesetter; Stephan Nagel, art director; Proof Positive/Farrowlyne Associates, Inc., front cover designer; Barbara Bartelson, back cover designer; Kate Mueller, cover illustrator; pre-press, printing, and binding by the graphics division of Saint Mary's Press.

Printed in the United States of America

Printing: 9 8 7 6 5 4 3 2 1

Year: 2007 06 05 04 03 02 01 00 99

ISBN: 0-88489-542-4

Contents

A Shard of Glass

by Carole Duncan Buckman

Rob, you just keep pressing that shard of glass into your heart, don't you?" As I tramped through the woods, the priest's words repeated in my head. "You're never going to be happy until you forgive him."

Forgive him. It'd be a cold day in hell when I forgave my father. Ten years ago he'd betrayed Mom, tearing apart our family. And now he had the nerve to be featured with his new family in the newspaper. In color. There he was, on the front page of last Sunday's "Life" section, the big oil man, in his designer home, hosting a charity party. Beside him was my stepmother with Morgan, my spoiled stepsister, conceived four months before my brother Jennings was born. Conceived while Dad was married to Mom. Why had I told Father Pete about it anyway? A shard of glass in my heart. That described the pain I felt when I thought about Dad.

I could live with it, couldn't I, that shard of glass? I wasn't all that unhappy. Girls hung around hoping I'd call. I was handsome, strong. I had a football scholarship as a kicker for UCLA in the fall. My school counselor had said that with my test scores, I could pursue any profession I wanted.

I kicked a rock, spinning it through the leaves. I lifted the backpack from my shoulders and reached for my water bottle. I'd taken a new path today, heading north from my house into the mountains. The woods were wilder here than along my usual route. It was nice hiking in the woods. Peaceful. It gave me time to think.

Father Pete is wrong. I don't have to forgive Dad. I can take his money and be civil, but I won't forget Dad's betrayal. And Dad knows it. Sure, he tried to explain. He didn't mean to break his marriage vows. He respected Mom, but he loved Sharon. Hypocrite!

Brush crunched behind me. I thought vaguely of wild animals, of mountain lions' teeth and claws. I started to turn. Then someone tackled me. I crashed to the ground, stunned. My face hit the forest floor. I inhaled mold, tasted acid in the damp leaves. Fists pummeled me. Boots kicked my ribs and legs. Men pulled off my backpack, my shirt. They took my boots and my pants with all the pockets. I couldn't fight back. They were all over me. I counted five of them, dark shadows, pulling and punching at me.

"You won't get away with this!" I shouted. I rolled over, intent on memorizing faces so I could identify them later. They were young, my age.

"Shut up!" the guy pawing through my bill-fold shouted. He swung his foot back and kicked toward my head.

I turned away, then felt stabbing pain on my neck. Colors flashed. My world went black.

A swirling wind blew that night, and leaves spiraled down, covering me. From time to time, I woke, confused, wondering if I was alive or if this helpless feeling was death. Through the black waving tree branches, I saw cold white stars. I wasn't cold. Like the rocks on the forest floor, I was unaffected by temperature. I tried to move my fingers. I couldn't feel them. My tears blurred the stars, and I closed my eyes. I hadn't cried since I was a child. What kind of man cried? I lapsed back into sleep.

When I opened my eyes again, shafts of sunlight bathed the forest. I listened to birds sing. A beige puppy stared into my face, then barked fiercely. I smelled wet dog. A boy bent over me. The boy's thick black hair needed cutting. He poked a stick at my cheek. I blinked fearfully as the stick moved toward my eyes. Please, God, save my eyes, I prayed.

"Hey, mister, are you alive?" the boy asked in Spanish.

"Ah," I said. I knew Spanish. I'd had perfect grades in Spanish. The words were there. Help me, I thought, but my tongue was frozen.

"Where are your clothes, mister? Aren't you cold in your underwear?" the boy asked.

"Ah," I said.

"You're all bloody. Wait here. I'll get my sister, María. She'll know what to do."

The boy and dog left. I listened to myself breathe. Birds called back and forth. A squirrel chattered. How long had it been since I'd left home Friday afternoon? "Gone hiking," my note had said. Mom would have found it on the kitchen table when she came in from work. She was used to my going off by myself. She encouraged my independence. I had a date with Jessica on Saturday night. Tonight. When I didn't show up, she'd be steamed. Would she call? Probably not. Too mad. She'd go out with the girls and cruise the drag.

Mom had a meeting in L.A. Monday morning. She'd think I'd gone to Dad's, wouldn't she? She might drop Jennings off at Dad's without asking if they knew where I was. I felt panic building in my chest.

The school attendance clerk would miss me. She'd call the house Monday. But Mom wouldn't return home to get the message until Wednesday. I could die by then, couldn't

I? Was my neck broken? Why couldn't I feel anything? What if the boy didn't come back?

I'm defenseless, I thought. The forest animals will find me. Rats, raccoons, ants, bugs. Mountain lions. Bobcats. If I lie here helpless, they may all come. Something rustled in the bushes. Senses. I can hear and see and smell. Is that good? If I'm about to be attacked again, I don't want to sense anything.

Oh, my God, I'm sorry for having sinned. Automatically I prepared for death. What were my sins? I'd been selfish, self-centered. I'd hurt Cindy when I dropped her after we'd dated for months. Dad, I'd never forgiven Dad. The shard of glass Father Pete had talked about. God, I forgive him. Do I mean it? If I don't mean it, it won't count. I want to mean it.

Forgive me as I forgive others. Dad was mostly good, wasn't he? He was wrong to betray Mom, but he was right in so many ways. Mom forgave him, didn't she? I remembered them laughing together over a joke at our shared Christmas dinner. In July Sharon and Dad had both flown to Washington for Grandpa's funeral, and they'd sat holding hands with the family, supporting us.

I thought of ski trips, of flying down mountains, leaping through moguls, daring Dad to follow, laughing when he crashed. Dad, gamely climbing back on his skis, always ready to try again.

Try again. How many times had Dad bought me whatever I wanted? And I'd never thanked him sincerely, had I? There'd always been that barrier—Thanks, but I still hate you.

I imagined my father standing in front of me. "Dad, I forgive you. I love you."

Then I thought of my stepsister, Morgan. I'd never taken her fishing when she wanted to go. I'd never done anything nice for her. I wished I had another chance to be a big brother to her.

I thought of Cindy, my old girlfriend. Why had I dropped her? I'd felt her love, hadn't I? And she'd been so much fun. But she'd wanted love back. It was easier for me to date lots of girls and never get too close. I wished I could tell her I was sorry.

I remembered a tall blond boy with thick glasses who sat in front of me in trig. He was new in school, and we'd all ignored him. It was probably hard to be new and not have any friends. I should have welcomed him. I should have tried to introduce him around, hung out with him.

The wind swirled more strongly, and leaves touched my face.

I imagined the UCLA football coach tramping up to me, carrying a football. "We expect you to keep up the kicking until fall, you know," he said. "You can't waste time lying here."

"I can't help it," I said.

"Well, then, someone else should have your scholarship."

"Yes, sir, that's fair," I said. The scholarship didn't seem important anymore. Football didn't seem important. The coach tramped away.

I felt light, as if I could float through the trees. The shard of glass was gone. I hadn't felt its going, but the pain was gone.

The rustling came nearer. Whatever it was, I was defenseless. God, I'll be a better person if You get me out of this, I promised. Then the woods were quiet again except for the cicadas and doves calling. I was alone, paralyzed and abandoned.

This was my cold day in hell. That's when I'd said I'd forgive. And I'd forgiven my father. Who else? The men who'd attacked me? I didn't want to die hating them. I forgave them, too. I smiled. Forgiving was easy.

I thought I saw Father Pete walking through the trees. He wore cowboy boots and his alb and stole.

"Can I have Communion, Father?" I asked. "The shard of glass is gone."

"And so you're happy?"

"Well, I guess, except I'm in trouble here."

Father leaned down and I tasted the bread. I felt Father's thumb anointing my forehead with oil. Deep peace filled me. Father Pete walked further into the forest.

I heard feet tramping through the brush.

"There you are, mister," the boy said. "Over here, María!"

The puppy licked my face. I felt the wet, rough tongue and smiled. Had I felt anything on my face before? Leaves, the stick? I couldn't remember. A teenage girl pushed the puppy away. Was she real? She was slight with black curling hair. She wore jeans and a faded navy blue sweatshirt.

"What happened to you?" she asked in Spanish.

"Ah," I answered.

"You shouldn't have come here," she said. "People are desperate."

The woods weren't far from home. Why shouldn't I be here?

Why were people desperate? This was California. Nobody was desperate in California. At least I'd never known it if they were. They were like the boy in trig, I thought, people I hadn't noticed. The guys who attacked me might have been illegals. People who needed money badly. The girl and her brother must be illegals, too, I thought. I couldn't expect them to help me.

"Can you move?" she asked.

I tried moving my fingers.

"I guess not," she said, tucking a blanket around me. Her cool fingers touched my face.

"I think your neck might be broken," she said. "Juan, run back and get that piece of plywood that's over the doorway. Wait until Ramon comes home from work and bring him, too." She turned back to me. "You're safe now. Sleep, if you want. I'll be here."

I closed my eyes and dozed. I dreamed that I was playing football. The cheerleaders were chanting my name. I imagined María standing under the bleachers, separated from me in the shadows.

It was dusk when I awoke. Cold raindrops fell on my face.

"Thank God, you've come, Ramon," María said.

A young Hispanic man stood over me. "Can he walk?" he asked.

"He can't move," she answered. "We need to put him on the plywood and get him to the shack before it really starts to rain."

"He'll be bringing *la migra* to us," Ramon said.

"Ramon, God sent him to us to help. We can't worry about getting caught," María said.

I watched Ramon put his arm around his sister. "You're always seeing God," he said.

They put the piece of wood down and lifted me. I heard the plywood scrape the forest floor. "Ah," I said, meaning please be careful. If you move my neck wrong, I'll die. The puppy barked and leaped in the leaves. The trees above me moved closer as I was lifted. I listened to the rain's gentle whisper and felt its cold tickle on my face.

"As soon as the rain stops, you need to run to the pay phone to call an ambulance. We can carry him to the highway to meet it," María said.

"I don't suppose he has any money on him," Ramon said.

"They took everything but his underwear."

"Ah," I said again. I have money at home. I'll pay you back for the phone call. I'll pay you for helping me.

"We can spare a quarter, Ramon," María said.

As if I were a babe in a cradle, I lay helpless on the board, rocked back and forth to the rhythm of their feet on the forest floor. I slept again. I awoke in a shack lit by a kerosene lamp. I smelled kerosene and food and people. The puppy's wet tongue licked my face. I stared up at the roof. Part of it was stone. The shack had been built onto a shallow cave. Tin and plywood pieced unevenly together served as the rest of the roof. María's family cast long shadows as they came one by one to stare down at me. A mother and father, a grandfather.

"Come, your dinner's ready," María's mother said.

"Let me give him more water and clean him up first, Mama," María answered.

I swallowed the liquid and watched her gently wipe my arm with the washcloth. She rinsed the cloth in a bucket, and I felt the warm water on my face, then pain when she touched my face above my eye. Pain is good, I thought. Feeling is good. She rinsed the washcloth.

"I have brothers," she said. "You don't need to be embarrassed."

How had she become so kind, so compassionate, I wondered? I fell asleep watching her.

I awoke to low voices speaking Spanish. The shack was mostly dark. I was being lifted on the plywood. I saw Ramon's back by the light of the kerosene lamp.

"It's all right," María said. "We'll get help."

Then I was outside, looking up at twisted tree branches and the stars, listening to their feet thud along the trail. The full moon lifted itself from behind a cloud. The trees still dripped and crackled from the rain, and the forest smelled fresh.

Suddenly the board lurched. The trees tilted.

"Ramon!" María shouted.

I closed my fingers over the edge of the plywood, held on. Or did I imagine my fingers moving? A pulse of hope throbbed in my heart.

"It's okay," Ramon said. "He didn't fall."

"Please be careful," María said.

When we reached the road, María sat cross-legged beside me on the ground. Cars and trucks came and went, their lights growing, growing, then with a roar disappearing. I smelled diesel, gasoline, exhaust.

"It won't take Ramon long to reach the pay phone. Then the ambulance will come," María said.

"Ah," I said. I dozed, then woke.

The ambulance lights pulsed red, and gravel crunched as the vehicle stopped beside me. María stood, a shadow in the headlights. Ramon had slipped away. The ambulance doors slammed.

"We found him hurt in the woods," María said.

"Hey, Jamison, you speak Spanish?" The uniformed man leaned over me.

"He can't move," María said. She pantomimed my neck breaking.

Another voice spoke. "She thinks his neck is broken. Heartbeat's good though, breathing good. I don't think he's hypothermic or dehydrated."

He spoke to me. "Okay, buddy, we're going to lift you into the ambulance. *Comprende?*"

"Grah," I said.

"Know his name?" Jamison asked in Spanish.

"No," María said.

"He must have been beaten up a few days ago. His cuts are already healing. What did you put on them?"

I remembered the leaves that had covered me. Healing leaves. Even then, God had been with me.

"You want to ride with us?" Jamison asked María.

"No, but I need the plywood and blanket," she answered.

I felt a collar being fitted around my neck. I was lifted from the plywood onto a stretcher, then into the ambulance.

María stood beside me with the blanket over her arm. Her hand touched my cheek.

"Vaya con Dios," she said. Go with God.

I will, I thought. The shard of glass was gone. I didn't know my future, but whatever happened, God would be with me. *"Gracias,"* I said.

The Volunteer

by Margaret Carlson

*J*enny banged the clock radio alarm down a split second before it was set to go off. She smiled. Few things in life gave her more pleasure than not hearing the wretched racket of her alarm clock at 5:30 in the morning. Jenny yawned and jumped out of bed, fully awake.

She showered, slipped into a gray plaid skirt and white blouse, and was out the door, grabbing a banana off the counter for breakfast before her mother or father or noisy sisters were out of bed. She pulled into the nearly empty parking lot of the Free Mart store. The store was run by the Little Sisters of the Poor, but it was Sister Nora's baby. Jenny parked her ten-year-old Toyota (bought with her father's help and her own money) and went to find Sister Nora.

"Morning, Sister," Jenny said to the huge nun standing between two teetering piles of clothes donated to the Free Mart. As usual, Sister Nora looked lost in her own store. "I'm here to help. What would you like me to do?"

"Oh, glory be! Jenny, am I glad to see you. Not that you wouldn't be here," she giggled. "Jenny Trumble, the most dependable teenager God created. And to think I was lucky enough to have Him send you to me! Praise the Lord."

Sister Nora glanced upward and smiled. She shifted her two-hundred-plus pounds east and west and leaned against a pile. "Oops," she said, steadying the clothes. "Feast or famine. It's always feast or famine around here, dear. Just look at all these nice things." Nora pushed a ladder next to the mountain of rags and dabbed her forehead with a hanky she had hidden in her sleeve.

"We're feasting today, praise the Lord." She stopped and let out a short, choppy giggle. Jenny sighed. Nothing about Nora suggested nun. She acted more like some of the clients that lined up for the rejects every day.

Probably it's the kind of thing that can happen to a person who stays in one place too long, Jenny thought. The shepherd starts acting like the sheep. She chuckled at her analogy. Anyhow, it wouldn't happen to her. She made certain to do her volunteering before the street people got there.

"You are such a dear," Nora babbled on. "Every day, here like clockwork, to give of yourself." Jenny waited silently for Nora to say what she should do. Sometimes the piles needed to be sorted by size and gender. But first, the rags had to be separated from the so-called good stuff.

Jenny never responded to Nora's praises. It wasn't necessary. Nora talked excessively and worried about everybody, including Father Steve, the staff at Saint Thomas, her fellow sisters, homeless people, alcoholics, drug addicts, pregnant teenagers, and Jenny. Of course Jenny didn't need Nora's concern. She had her life well under control.

"I don't mind sorting out the rags," Jenny said, smiling. She was tired of waiting for Nora. She had to leave for school in an hour. If she was to get any work done, she had to start. "As a matter of fact, Sister, I like doing this kind of work. I can think and plan my day." Jenny thought a minute and added, "And pray."

"Of course you don't mind. That's just like our Jenny. Thank you, thank you, dear," Sister Nora said, wobbling away and finally leaving Jenny to her solitude.

Digging through strangers' castoffs was not Jenny's idea of a good time. But she was a Christian, and any fool knew a good Christian helped people who were less fortunate than themselves. And the people who showed up for freebies were a lot less fortunate than she was. They smelled bad. They had rotten teeth. Their kids had runny noses. Jenny couldn't imagine how they could live like that.

Of course it didn't hurt to be able to list a bunch of "good deeds" on her college applications. Jenny was headed to an Ivy League college. The best schools looked at more than test scores and class placement. Jenny planned to give them plenty to look at.

One hour later Jenny was pulling into West High School. Finding a parking spot was not as easy as it had been at the Free Mart. Jenny wasn't the first to arrive, but she wasn't the last either. Most of her classmates liked to wait until the last minute, and then speed through the lot like maniacs and park in No Parking spots. Crazy drivers! They were all jocks anyhow, and nobody would blame them for being stupid.

At lunch hour Jenny met her best friend and the second-biggest person she knew. Jenny and Darcy couldn't have looked less similar. Jenny was skinny. Darcy was fat. Jenny wore thick glasses, she had bad skin, and her poorly cut hair was short and curly. Darcy's hair was long, flat, and blonde, and it drooped over her fleshy pink face. She had watery blue eyes, but at least she didn't need glasses. Jenny had to admit that it was their physical shortcomings that brought them together. She knew that the kids called them Laurel and Hardy behind their backs, but she didn't care.

One day Jenny would be a famous neuro-surgeon or Supreme Court justice. She hadn't decided which yet. Then she'd be the one laughing. Jenny planned on being class val-edictorian, too. Only Tyler Jefferson was putting holes in that plan. Who would have predicted that the dumbest kid in her grade school would turn into a genius? A "black male" genius! Not that Tyler's race mattered. That'd be racist thinking, and what racist would ever work at the Free Mart?

"What's wrong?" Darcy said, pushing into the seat across from Jenny.

"Nothing. Why?"

Darcy smiled, releasing half a dozen dim-ples. "You had a real pained look on your face. Like you got an A on your English pa-per and Tyler got an A+."

"Geez, Darcy, sometimes you act so juve-nile," Jenny snapped. "What makes you think I care what Tyler Jefferson does?"

Darcy shrugged, "Forget it. How's Sister Nora?" She unglued the cellophane stuck to her cheeseburger and took a sloppy bite.

"Same as ever," Jenny said, glad that Darcy had changed the subject. "She's CLD."

"CLD?" Darcy repeated.

"Confused, Lost, and Disheveled," Jenny said, laughing. She peeled the banana she'd forgotten to eat for breakfast and removed the black tips from the ends. Eating the banana helped defuse the assault Darcy's lunch was making on her nose. Jenny wished that Darcy would eat less, or at least better, like she did. Darcy didn't have one iota of self-control.

"Nora's a funny old bird," Jenny said. "Maybe a nun's habit would help her to act more like a nun."

"Get real, girl. Besides, I like her," Darcy said, rolling a rubbery French fry in a plastic cup of ketchup. "She always has something nice to say. And she means it, too. One time when I was helping at the Free Mart, a lady came in with five raggedy little kids, all looking and smelling like they'd slept in the streets for weeks. Nora made the mother sit in the back room. She brought her coffee." Darcy smiled. "Anyhow, she took those kids one at a time, gave each one a shopping bag, and filled those bags with the best stuff in the joint. Nora treated those kids like they were shopping at Macy's. Then she took the family for pie at the coffee shop next door."

"We're not supposed to do that," Jenny said stiffly.

"I know that, Jenny, but you know how Nora is. She can't help her niceness. Anyhow," Darcy said, cheerily, "they all came back looking a lot happier."

"It's the principle," Jenny argued. "We aren't supposed to buy them food or other things. Rules are rules! They're put there for a reason."

Darcy frowned. "What reason is that?"

Jenny and Darcy locked eyes.

"Come on, Jen, let's not fight about it."

She was right. It was foolish wasting time arguing as if she cared what Sister Nora did.

"Okay, Darcy," Jenny nodded. "What are you doing Saturday?"

"Why?"

"I'm going to the Rec Center to help Randy set up for the volleyball tournament. We could use some help."

"I'd love to, Jenny, but I promised my mom I'd help her with the kids." Darcy licked her fingers. "She has some stuff she wants to do."

"Can't your dad help her?"

"He's out of town."

"He's always out of town," Jenny said. "Honestly, I don't see why you always have to baby-sit. I mean, you're eighteen. You're entitled to your own life. They tie you down."

"You know Dad's a salesman. Besides, I have my own life." Darcy shook her head. "I happen to like my sibs. So it'd be dumb for my parents to waste money on a sitter when I'm perfectly willing to baby-sit." The bell rang. Darcy started crunching wrappers into a pile. "And I'm not tied down," she said angrily. Then, as if regretting her words, she added, "If the tournament is still on next week, I'll be glad to help."

"Great," Jenny said, standing. Darcy always called for a truce before departing. Jenny was glad, but she also knew that Darcy would never risk permanently antagonizing the only person who tolerated her size. "Call me later?"

After school Jenny found her mother in the kitchen with the twins, Ellen and Mayme, hanging on her skirt. They were both shouting, "Me! Me!" as usual.

"Hi, Mom," Jenny said. "What's for dinner?"

"Chili. How was school today?"

"Boring."

"I'm sorry to hear that. I could use a boring day," her mom said, patting Ellen on the head. Or was it Mayme? No matter, it was a horse apiece with those two. "What was boring about school?"

Jenny rolled her eyes. Only her mother would ask what was boring about school. She left for the den.

"Would you mind taking the twins, dear?" Her mother called after her. "They've been underfoot all day. I haven't been able to get a thing done."

Reluctantly, Jenny scooped up the girls. Laundry, the vacuum cleaner, and toys were scattered everywhere, making her mother's words of explanation unnecessary. After dinner Jenny did her homework, thinking, not for the first time, that she would have only one child.

On Saturday Jenny arrived at the Rec Center early so that she could put up the net without the unhelpful help of overexcited preteens. She was almost done when she heard the activity director, Randy. She knew it was Randy because he was always singing, and the person coming was struggling with the low notes of "Summertime." Any second he would pop around the corner and ask how she expected to play volleyball in a skirt, or comment about the man's work she was doing, or say something stupid about her hair. Randy never said "Hi," like a regular person.

"Well, look it that, will ya," Randy said, flashing a perfect set of Hollywood teeth. Randy's brown face had more dimples than Darcy's, and his eyelashes were so long they looked fake. Jenny was the only female at the center who was not charmed by Randy.

"I say nobody, and I means nobody, be's more dedicated to de Rec Center than little Miss—oops, I means Ms. Trumble!"

Jenny shook her head disgustedly. "Knock it off, Randy."

"Yessum," he said, smiling. Jenny hated it when he acted like Step'n Fetchit. Old-time movie buffoons were a disgrace to his people, and he should know better than to imitate them.

"Seriously, how long have you been here?" Randy asked. "Here, let me help you with that," he said, grabbing a section of the rope and tying it in place. When the net was up, Randy said, "Hey, Jenny, I wasn't kidding. You really are dependable. And you need to know that I appreciate the time you give." Jenny was embarrassed, and she couldn't hold back her smile. Randy nodded. "I'll go turn on the scoreboard."

When everything was ready, Randy called Jenny into his office.

"Have a seat," he said, as Jenny entered. In the two years that Jenny had volunteered at the Rec Center, Randy had never asked her in for a conference. She couldn't imagine what he wanted. She found a chair under a pile of sports magazines. She pushed the magazines aside, her curiosity piqued.

"I was talking about you the other day. Saying how smart you be," Randy said, smiling like a devil on a mission. "I hope my characterization be's accurate?"

"That is a big word, Randy. *Characterization.* But yes, I am smart. To whom were you speaking?"

Randy's smile widened. "Tia!" Jenny waited. He wanted to play guessing games. She didn't.

"You know, she's the girl with the beads in her braids. Plays a mean game of V-ball."

"So what?" Jenny said, folding her arms in frustration. "Get to the point."

"I told her I'd talk to you about maybe helping her a bit," Randy said, twirling a pen with a basketball eraser on it. "Yesterday she sat in a corner of the gym crying. She didn't even practice, and you know how important volleyball is to . . ."

"Stop," Jenny interrupted. "Let me guess. Her father beats her mother? Or how about her father beats her? Or better yet, her mother's a drug addict?"

Randy wrinkled his nose.

"She needs help with her math. Her mom tries, but Tia says her mom doesn't know how to do it. Her teacher says she hasn't got time. She told Tia to get outside help. Like Tia can afford to hire a tutor! Ask me, the teacher should take a long walk off a short pier." Randy stopped and smiled sheepishly. "Sorry, guess I lose patience when I see these kids get raw deals. So, whatdoyasay?"

"I say, I hope you didn't promise anything."

"I didn't actually, but I think she sort of read it like a promise. She's a kid, and you know kids. She got all excited when I said I'd ask. I don't think she heard much after that."

"You shouldn't have said anything, Randy. I can't do it."

"Why not? Is it a matter of time? Because if it is, no problem. You can do it when you come here."

"It's not the time," Jenny said. "I'm not a social worker."

"Nobody said you were."

"I'm not a tutor either," Jenny said, through clenched teeth. "I work at the Free Mart, at my church, at school, and here, not to mention everything I have to do at home. My time is planned." Jenny rubbed her hands and diverted her eyes from Randy's. "What gives you the right to interfere?"

Randy didn't answer. He stared past her and studied his pen for what seemed like hours. Jenny preferred his shucking and jiving. The silence threatened to swallow her alive. Finally, Randy put the pen down carefully and looked straight into her eyes.

"Why do you do it?"

"Do what?" Jenny asked, still angry at his lack of consideration.

"Volunteer."

Family Meeting

by Vivian C. M. Markert

*E*lliot heard his dad's footsteps, the unhurried, measured strides, advancing down the hallway. It was unusual for his dad to approach Elliot's private domain. Usually he just shouted up the steps.

Elliot wondered if he should turn off his computer game. That way his dad wouldn't lecture him on that "incredible waste of time." On the other hand, this *was* Elliot's room. So he waited, fingers deliberately hovering over his keyboard, until his father knocked politely, twice.

"Come on in," Elliot said.

His father just stuck his head in the door. "Hi, Son. I'd apologize for interrupting, but I see you're just . . . ah . . ."

"Wasting my time?" Elliot said gravely. He was rewarded with an appreciative gleam in his father's eyes.

"I can tell I'm wearing out *that* particular complaint. Anyhow, I'm calling a family meeting in ten minutes. Okay with you?"

Elliot shrugged and said, "Sure. Problem?"

"Come and find out," his father said. Then, hesitatingly, "I hope it's not. A problem, that is." He smiled uncertainly and left.

Well, well, Elliot thought. *That* was different. Usually his dad would just say, "Family meeting! Be there or be square!" For as long as Elliot could remember, family meetings were called for two reasons: one was to discuss issues and take votes, like on family vacations, chore assignments, or discipline issues; the other was to announce a big family event like a wedding or something.

Maybe that was it, another family baptism or confirmation or first Communion or whatever, Elliot mused as he saved his game. That would be okay. He tried to hurry, but by the time he got downstairs, Elliot found he was the last one in the den and wound up sitting on the floor, with his back to the unlit fireplace.

His father sat on one of the bar stools, towering over the rest of them. His mother sat in the recliner, a small half smile firmly in place, her hands clenched in her lap. She looked nervous, plain and simple.

Maybe she was going out East to take care of Grandma again. That would explain his father's apologetic glance earlier, because they all hated dividing up Mom's chores to do when she was gone. Or maybe they were

short of money again and were going to
have to scale down summer vacation plans.
. . . That would be okay with him. *He*
hadn't voted for going all the way to Boston
to visit boring relatives. He'd voted for loaf-
ing a week or two at a lake cabin. But his
parents prided themselves on family democ-
racy. It had been four against one on that
vote.

Elliot's two younger sisters sat at polar op-
posites on the couch, Gloria nearest Mom,
Celeste—known as Sissy—nearest Dad. They
looked mystified, too. Mom, as usual, started
the meeting.

"Okay, kids. We're all here, and your father
has something to share with you."

"Well, no one's in trouble, if that's what
you're wondering," Dad said. "I've got an an-
nouncement to make, that's all. Big changes
are afoot, so hang on to your hats."

Elliot risked a quick glance at his mother.
Her smile had become even more fixed. A
little apprehensive now, he turned his gaze
back to his father in time to catch the closing
of his next sentence.

". . . new corporate headquarters in Sili-
con Valley. How about that? I've been given
the opportunity to head the sales office there.
It's what I've always dreamed of. I'd have the
regional salespeople reporting directly to me.
Lots more responsibility. *Lots* more money.

What do you think of that?" Dad paused. And smiled. The girls just gave each other quick, confused looks. Dad's eyes locked with Elliot's.

Elliot felt his mouth go suddenly dry. "You're talking about moving. Is that it, Dad? Moving out to California?"

Gloria squealed with all her eleven-year-old might. "Disneyland! Do you mean THAT California?" Sissy clapped her hands together, mimicking her sister's delight.

"When?" Elliot asked, ignoring them.

"This summer, Champ," Dad answered, that apologetic tone back in his voice. "No later than July if we can help it."

Elliot tried to keep his voice even.

"Dad, that's the summer before my senior year. I do not want to move before my senior year."

His sisters quieted, looking at him solemnly.

"Don't you want to go?" Sissy asked.

He turned his attention to her. Safer this way.

"No, Sissy. I don't."

Her chubby seven-year-old face mirrored his in frowns.

"Why not?"

"All my friends are here, Sissy. I'm on student council. Orchestra's been working for our senior trip to Washington for two years.

And my girlfriend is here, Monica, you remember her, right?

Sissy brightened. "She's nice!"

Elliot just shrugged helplessly at that. He
didn't know what to say.

Into the silence Mom said quietly, "I understand, Elliot. We knew this would be hardest
on you. But if your father doesn't take this
opportunity now, then it may be years before he gets another chance. If ever."

Elliot shook his head. "Why doesn't he
commute for a year? Dad? Why don't you fly
home on weekends? And vacations?"

"Who says I'll be free on the weekends?
Don't you think I've thought of that, Elliot?"
Dad said. "The first year in a new job is very
stressful. I'll have to be ready for working
weekends, vacations . . . commuting just
won't work."

"And we want the family to stay together,"
Mom added. "You know how important it is
to your father and me that we all stay together."

Then Sissy broke in with a stupid question about bringing the dog, Gloria bounced
around in her excitement, and the attention
was off Elliot.

He sat there in numbed silence. Inside him
a bubble of anger grew. What was going on,
anyway? Why even call a family meeting to

discuss this? This wasn't a discussion. His parents were just *telling* them that they were moving. Why even pretend that the power in this situation was shared, because it wasn't. Not by a long shot. Elliot closed his eyes, trying to regain some control. He breathed deeply.

Still, his voice came out too loud when he finally said: "I'm not going. That's it. You can't mess up my senior year. You can't." When no one said anything, he abruptly stood up and fled, making it to the door in three big strides.

"Oh, Elliot, please don't leave," Mom said, a pleading look on her face.

That stopped him. He suddenly remembered how excited *she* had been about the big orchestra trip, volunteering to chaperone and everything.

Then his father said, "Sit down, Son. The meeting's not over yet." Elliot turned to face him but kept his hand on the door.

"It's not? You mean we really get a vote here? Majority rules?"

He had the satisfaction of watching his father's face turn red. "I didn't think so," Elliot muttered and left, quickly, ignoring whatever it was his mother was calling out to him.

Hesitating outside the door, he considered what to do. Go back upstairs? Call Monica?

Or maybe go over to her house? But it was Wednesday, and she baby-sat her younger sister on Wednesdays. He couldn't go over there. And somehow he didn't want to tell her the bad news over the phone.

He'd go talk to Franklin. If anyone could help, it would be his best friend since kindergarten. Elliot tiptoed through the house and slipped outside. He paused there, taking deep breaths, allowing the sharp March night air to cool his face and the hot lump in his throat. He certainly didn't want to act like a fool at the Adderly's house. Then he picked his way through the back lilacs, jumped the Adderly's fence, and knocked on their back door.

Soon enough he was ensconced in Franklin's room and had spilled his story in a semi-garbled rush.

Franklin stared at him. "Unbelievable. Have you told Monica yet?"

"No. I'll wait until I see her. I thought of e-mailing her, but she'd read it late tonight . . . seems kind of a bad way to tell her."

"Is there a good way?"

They sat in silence for a minute or so. Then Franklin said, "Kind of weird. I mean, to have your parents just step in and take everything away from you. How about college? You've already picked Saint Augustine's. Will this change all that too? Man, we're supposed to room together."

Elliot groaned. "I hadn't even thought that far ahead. I wonder if my folks have."

"And another thing!" Now Franklin's voice sounded mad too. "I thought your family was big on voting on things. I always thought that was awesome. Don't you get any say in this at all?"

"Nope. That's why I had to get out of there. I was so mad, I was afraid I'd . . . don't know . . . explode." And he still felt that way.

"I wouldn't blame you," Franklin said. "Nothing's worse than feeling like nothing you say or do is going to make any difference." Franklin was making him feel even worse, if that was possible. Elliot's dismay must have shown on his face because Franklin grimaced and said, "Sorry. I'm not helping. It's just that in one more year, you'd have been scot-free. Too bad you couldn't just stay here with us, you know, like that time your parents went to that out-of-town funeral. Remember?"

"Yeah. I remember. That was okay." Elliot got up restlessly and moved around Franklin's room. He picked up a trophy and set it down again. The silence stretched; Elliot found himself avoiding Franklin's eyes.

Franklin suddenly said, "Are you thinking what I'm thinking?"

Elliot shrugged helplessly. "Come on, Frank. When you said that, you didn't mean it seriously."

"That's how great ideas come to people, Elliot. Out of the blue."

"How in the world could we ask your parents? I wouldn't even know how to start. 'Hi, Mr. and Mrs. Adderly, can I stay here for a year? I'll help take the garbage out.' Geez."

"There's only one way to do something like that," Franklin said, heading for the door. "Just do it."

"You're kidding, right?" Elliot couldn't believe his ears, but for the first time, a faint thread of hope began to weave itself around his heart. "You think we should just go down there and . . . what?"

"Not us. Me." Franklin grinned again. "Only-child syndrome. I'm spoiled rotten, and I don't want you to see my technique here."

Elliot couldn't help grinning back. "Go for it."

The second Franklin shut the door behind him, Elliot regretted the impetuousness of their idea. It seemed such a huge thing to ask . . . too huge. He sat down heavily on Franklin's bed and flopped back, his feet still on the floor. He covered his eyes with one arm. He couldn't help wondering what was

going on back home. Had his folks gone upstairs and found his empty room? Were they
mad? He tried to imagine what his senior year
would be like in a new school, one where
absolutely no one knew him. All the groups
would have been formed years before. There
would be nowhere to fit in.

Then the door burst open, and Franklin
was back. Elliot sat up quickly. Franklin's face
was flushed; he wore a big grin.

"You're not going to believe this," he said.
"My folks think it's a real possibility. You'll
just have to get your folks to agree. Listen
. . ." Franklin pulled a chair opposite Elliot.
He sat down and leaned forward, his words
tumbling out now. "Listen, they went for the
whole thing. They even mentioned the spare
room that we just stack junk in. You could
help me clean it out this summer, paint
it. . . . Mom's been nagging Dad and me to
do that for years."

Elliot had been slowly nodding at his
words.

"This is crazy. They just went for it like
that?" He felt his heart beat faster with something like real joy.

"Mom said we practically live at each other's houses anyway, what difference would it
make? Dad thinks it's a good idea too,
only . . ." Franklin hesitated. "Only he says
that it's your place to, you know, ask your

parents. He says this can't be done without your parents' 'full cooperation.'"

Elliot's immediate elation disappeared.

"That's the big if, isn't it?"

Franklin gave him a crooked smile.

"Worth a try, Elliot. You don't lose anything by asking them."

"It would be strange, though, my family in California and me here."

"Not so strange," Franklin said. "It would only be a year from next fall and you would be leaving for college anyway. You'd be gone anyway."

"My dad said he wants to keep the family together no matter what."

Franklin frowned.

"Don't argue their side, Elliot. It's your life too. Listen, my dad says you shouldn't decide right now. He says you should think it over without undue influence from any outside party, meaning me, I guess." Franklin's eyes sparkled. "But hey, what are friends for? Right?"

"Right." Elliot stood up. "I'd better get back. I want to talk to them tonight. If I wait until tomorrow, I may lose my nerve."

Franklin took him downstairs, where Elliot spent an awkward moment thanking the Adderlys. Walking him out, Franklin shook his hand briefly at the door.

"Do what you've got to do," he said to Elliot's murmured thanks.

Elliot slowly walked through the dark to his own back porch. Instead of going in, though, he sat down on the porch swing. He still couldn't believe the Adderlys' suggestion. He couldn't believe his problem was practically solved. So why did he still feel that lump in his chest?

He hunkered down on the swing and considered the Adderlys' invitation, which suddenly felt like a new problem. He didn't know what was bothering him about it. The Adderlys were his parents' good friends too. His mom and Mrs. Adderly were always joining school committees together. It wasn't like the Adderlys were coming out of left field or anything. And Franklin's mom was right; they had been practically living in each other's houses for how many years now? Forever.

This should be automatic. He should be able to just march in and tell his parents what he wanted to do. But, he realized with sudden insight, maybe the decision *wasn't* that automatic. What *did* he really want to do? To go or to stay?

He didn't know. Having a choice felt almost worse than *not* having one.

Closing his eyes, Elliot let pictures and thoughts just float in his brain. His parents were so big on family togetherness. He knew it would hurt them a lot if he did leave them a year early. Like on Sundays, the whole family always went to church together, Elliot checking ahead to find out which Mass Father Tony was preaching, because that would be the best one . . . and Mom and Dad would humor him on that. Funny to think about their Sundays together being numbered.

But they'd be numbered even if he did go to California with them. No matter what, eventually Elliot would be leaving home. He'd be on his own. No more Monday night football with his dad. No more taking the girls out trick-or-treating. No more impromptu family hikes at the nature center . . . late-night secret Dairy Queen raids with his mom . . . long, loud political discussions at the dinner table.

Elliot tried to picture himself at college . . . separate from the rest of them. Independent but also alone. Was he really ready for that? The lump in his throat grew larger.

A mess, that's what this all was. A mess created by Dad. Elliot felt his resentment toward his father come swelling back up. If he sacrificed his senior year for his dad's desire to keep the family together these added months, he'd just wind up resenting them, wouldn't he? Elliot stopped the swing with one downturned foot.

He could mull things over forever, and it still wouldn't matter, he knew, because when he got right down to it, he didn't know if his parents would even *let* him decide anything.

He looked up again at the sky. A sliver of moon was peeking through the bare branches of the lilacs. Lord, but he was tired. He blinked, and the moon swam a bit before sharpening back into its curved lines. He swiped at the corners of his eyes.

From inside the house, he could hear the deeper murmur that was his dad's voice. He must be sitting in the kitchen, close by. Mom would be there too. They'd be waiting in the kitchen for him, all right, both of them, chairs turned so that they could watch the back door. They would have guessed he'd gone to Franklin's house.

They were waiting for him to come home.

Standing, Elliot took a deep breath and stretched. The heavy lump in his chest was gone. He had figured at least one thing out. He wouldn't go in there all angry and ready to dictate his terms. He wouldn't go in there with an attitude . . . if he could help it. He'd go in there ready to talk.

Because it was time for another family meeting. Only this time the meeting would be just between his parents and him. This time there'd be no voting, no majority rules.

Just talking. And listening. Like maybe all the other family meetings had been practice for this time, for this one time, when they really did have to meet as equals, when he would tell them how he felt and what he really needed.

And maybe he just had to have a little faith that in the end they'd work things out. Together.

Mountains of the Moon

by Carol Estes

Black is what brings out the stars, Maggie. It's simple physics." My brother, Stanley, and I lay on an old blue quilt we'd spread over the dry grass behind the barn, and stared into a sky as clear as black glass.

"See, Maggie, starlight goes hurtling through outer space at millions of miles per hour for years and years, just to get to the place where you and I see it tonight." When Stanley turned his face toward me, his eyes seemed almost as black as the sky. "You with me so far, kiddo?"

I was.

"Okay. These beams of starlight are weak and delicate after traveling all that way, and the bright lights on earth easily outshine them. That's why you can't see the stars in the daytime. A clear black sky away from the lights of the city is what brings out the stars." Stanley folded his arms behind his head. I was happy lying beside him, listening to his stories and the familiar rhythm of his shallow, difficult breathing, secretly studying him. The night was full of rustlings in the dry grass and thousands of cricket legs rubbing together in the flat acres around us.

"Just think, Maggie, right here, tonight, in the middle of nowhere, with no light for miles around, you and I can see the stars better than most people in the world."

The summer of 1962 was scorching hot and dry as dust. By noon it was usually too hot to stay inside, so when I wasn't in the basement with Stanley, I sat under the plum tree in the yard with Mama, drinking lemonade. Mama did mending or snapped string beans into the blue metal bowl in her lap—thunk, thunk, thunk. Or sometimes she just sat and stared at the horizon, fanning herself with a cardboard fan that said "Rankin Funeral Home" on the back.

"Go see how hot it is, Maggie," she'd say. "I bet a dollar it's over a hundred again." I'd run across the sharp brown grass, my sandals flopping against the soles of my feet, to check the thermometer on the barn door, scaring up flights of grasshoppers from the tall weeds as I ran.

"You won another dollar!" I'd yell back. If Mama's bets had paid off, she'd have won twenty-three dollars that summer—the hottest on record in Clark County, Kansas.

Nights were cooler than the days, but the house was still too hot for sleeping. No air moved through the upstairs bedrooms on the east side, where Stanley and I slept. It was cooler on the west, where Pa slept, because of the breeze, but Pa said that was fair since he was the only one putting in a decent day's work.

One night I tried pushing my bed in front of the window, but the old iron frame made so much noise scraping across the wooden floor that I was afraid of waking Pa. I woke Stanley instead, because he tiptoed into my room a few minutes later with his shoes in one hand and the quilt in the other. That was the first night I spent outside with him, listening to stories about the constellations and the ancient Greeks.

Stanley was different from the rest of us Larsens, like the one stalk of milo that grows twice as tall as a thousand others in the same field and makes you wonder what seed it came from. He was dark and mysterious, the way I imagined a gypsy would be, with black hair that hung down across his forehead and shone with bluish highlights in the sun. His black eyes were so dark you couldn't even see the pupils, and he had long thick lashes. He was taller than Pa but frail looking, with white skin and girlish features.

Once I asked Mama what was wrong with Stanley.

"Allergies. You know that. He's allergic to everything—dust, pollen, and especially wheat and wheat dust. Kansas is a lousy place to raise a boy who's allergic to dust."

"Stanley said one time he quit breathing and passed out when he was shoveling wheat and had to go to the hospital in Dodge City."

"That's how we found out what was wrong with him."

"Is that why Pa says he's allergic to work?"

"That's just one of Pa's jokes that's not funny."

"Pa says Stanley will make someone a lovely wife."

"That's not funny, either."

"Is Pa his real father?"

"Maggie! Who puts these crazy notions in your head?"

"No one. I just thought Stanley might be a gypsy."

Mama laughed. "I swear, Maggie! What an imagination."

"Like the ancient Greeks," I said mysteriously.

At noon Mama and I drove the truck out into the field to bring Pa sandwiches and sweating quart jars full of ice water. Pa still used an ancient tractor and the old one-way plow, years after neighbors like the Gillises had switched to new tractors that had air-conditioning and adjustable seats. When he saw us coming, he left the tractor idling, heat waves rising from the motor, and walked across the plowed ground to meet us. He sat down on the tailgate, his face and neck flushed and covered with black dirt and sweat. He dipped his kerchief in one of the jars of cold water and wiped the dirt off his face, then handed it to me.

"Get this wet again, Maggie." I took the muddy scarf, swished it in the water, and handed it dripping back to him.

"How come we don't get one of those new tractors like Gary Gillis has, Pa?" I asked. "The kind with air-conditioning."

Mama shot me a warning look.

"Because the Larsens like to do things the old-fashioned way? That's what Stanley says."

"Oh, he does, does he?" Pa poured ice water from a second mason jar down his throat so fast it ran down both sides of his chin. He wiped his mouth with his sleeve.

"Gary Gillis is in hock up to his armpits. Doesn't know it yet, but he's sold his soul to the devil. Hell, he's not a real farmer anymore. He might as well be sitting in the cockpit of an airplane."

"Pa, I just meant that maybe we should join the twenty-first century, like Stanley says."

Pa squinted at me and I could see that I was making things worse.

"So you and the little lord of the manor think you've got it pretty rough." Pa grabbed my arm. His wet fingers pressed hard into my skin. "You don't know what rough is." Then Pa let go and stomped back across the furrows. He climbed up on the tractor seat.

"Can't you take a break for lunch, Leo?" Mama called. "You shouldn't be plowing in this heat."

Pa acted like he didn't hear her.

I liked spending time in the cool basement with Stanley. He'd be going away to the university in the fall to study physics and astronomy, and, he said, to prepare himself physically and mentally for outer space.

Pa said Stanley would never make it as an astronaut, but Pa didn't know everything. He didn't know that Stanley did fifty push-ups and a hundred sit-ups every day, or that he was building a telescope in the basement, or that he was planning to be the first man on the moon. Only Stanley and I knew that.

Stanley jumped when he finally noticed me sitting on the stool next to him.

"Darn it, Maggie!"

"Ha! Scared you. How's the telescope coming?"

Stanley turned back to his work.

"Okay, I guess. Slow." He had laid all the parts out in meticulous order on the workbench. Some pieces were held together with small clamps.

"When do we get to look through it?"

"Pretty soon." He held a piece up to the light and examined it, brushing his hair out of his eyes with his other hand.

"What will we see?" I'd asked him this before, but I liked hearing his answers. He held another piece up to the light. "Spaceships?" I prompted. Stanley smiled.

"Not likely. Let's see. We'll see the mountains of the moon."

"What are they like?"

"Real mountains, just like the Rockies. Not snowcapped, of course."

"What else?"

Stanley put down the lens so that he could use his hands to demonstrate. "Meteors, maybe. Remember I told you that falling stars are really sizzling meteors, burning up in earth's atmosphere?"

"Yep."

"Well, there's no atmosphere on the moon, see, so the meteors don't burn up. They just fall out of the sky at tremendous speeds—

BAM!" Stanley demonstrated with a sponge and smashed it into the workbench. "Imagine that—rocks the size of mountains that shake the whole moon when they hit, and shoot rooster tails of dust clear into outer space." He drew a graceful rooster tail in the air.

"Dust?" I said, with a tight feeling in my stomach. "A lot of dust?" But Stanley went right on.

"And get this, Maggie. When we think we see a star, we really don't. We're looking at light from the star that started beaming toward us years and years ago and finally got close enough for us to see it. Nobody's ever really seen the stars. Only the light."

"How could that be?" I asked skeptically.

"Trust me." Stanley squinted one eye shut and looked through a lens. "Now get lost, so I can concentrate."

The yard light was a surprise to everyone but Pa. Stanley had gone to Dodge City for his doctor's appointment the day the truck from Klaussen's Electric in Minneola pulled into the yard. A man with "Klaussen's" in red letters on his shirt and a leather tool belt slung around his hips came to the back door. Pa met him on the back porch. I saw them and followed Mama into the kitchen.

"What's going on, Mama?"

"Hush!" She leaned toward the open window above the sink. I could see Pa and the electrician talking outside the window, and Pa pointing at the electrical pole by the barn. The electrician went to his van, and Pa came inside, letting the screen door slam.

"What's the electrician doing here?" Mama said. Pa was a big man, and he always stood straight. When he stood in the kitchen doorway, even in those last years, his shoulders seemed to block the light.

"I bought us a yard light."

"Yard light!" Mama and I said in unison.

"Leo! When there's so many things we really need!" Mama looked out the window in disbelief. I could see the man dragging a spool of cable from the van.

"What do we need a yard light for, Pa?" I asked.

"It'll light up the whole place as bright as day. Keep criminals away."

"We can't afford it," Mama said quietly.

"I already decided we can afford it. It's done."

"I guess maybe you're getting forgetful in your old age. Guess you forgot we only harvested twenty bushels to the acre this year."

"Don't tell me what we harvested."

"Then I guess you forgot we're going to have to squeeze every blessed penny we've got just to keep food on the table."

Pa clenched his fist but brought it down against the doorjamb in slow motion.

He said quietly, "I'm sick of remembering what we can't afford, Mary. I decided to do this and it's done."

The Klaussen's man pulled a big carton from the van and tore it open.

"What's the matter with you, anyway?" said Pa. "I thought you all wanted to be modern like the Gillises." Mama wouldn't look at him now. Pa shrugged and pulled his red seed cap tight over his forehead. "Well, now we're modern." He let the back door slam behind him.

For a long time Mama stood at the sink, looking out the window. Finally she saw me watching her.

"Go help your Pa, Maggie," she said, annoyed. "Go on."

I found Pa in the barn with the tractor. It was dark and dusty there, but this time of year, it smelled like fresh-cut prairie hay.

"Need any help, Pa?"

"No."

"Mama said I should help you. She was just trying to get rid of me, though."

Pa got out a metal toolbox, set it down next to the tractor, and slid underneath.

"All right, then, you hand me the tools when I tell you to. First the big wrench." I handed him the biggest wrench I could find. "Too big." I tried another.

"Pa, these stalls are really for horses instead of cows, aren't they?"

"We had horses when I was a kid," he said from under the tractor. "Workhorses that pulled a plow, not them fancy riding horses."

"Did you ever ride them?"

"Do you ever stop talking?"

"Come on, Pa! Did you ride them?"

"Sometimes I rode them out to the fields to be hitched up. To school a couple times. Hand me that big pan."

"Did you have horses in all the stalls?"

"Most of 'em."

"Tell me their names, Pa. Please!"

"Let's see, there was Bob in that first stall there by the door, then Peg, then a mare named Sara, a pretty chestnut named Blaze that never was good for much, and old Robroy there on the end, father of all the rest. Now I'm gonna slide this oil pan out to you. You take it out behind the barn."

I carried it carefully, trying not to slosh the oil, past the stalls where I could almost see Sara, Blaze, and Robroy stomping and snorting, and poured it on the ground out back. Pa was standing next to the tractor when I returned, fiddling with the motor.

"Was Peg short for Pegasus?" I asked him.

"What? No. Peg Leg. He had one white sock."

"I'm going to wish for a horse on my birthday. If I get him, I'm going to name him Pegasus."

"What's that supposed to mean?"

"Never mind. What happened to all the horses?"

"Well, old Robroy just keeled over one day. Old age, I guess. The others I shot."

"Shot! Why?"

"They got too old to work. Everything and everybody has to earn its keep on a farm. You can put an old horse out to pasture for a time, but sooner or later you're going to have to shoot him. It's a kindness in the long run."

"No, Pa!" I said, starting to cry. "I could never shoot Pegasus."

"You'd be surprised what you can do if you have to, Maggie. Now quit your bellyaching or go on back inside with your mother."

I waited on the back porch that evening to watch the new light come on and to see what Stanley would say when he got home. At dusk the light began to glow purple, and gradually it lit the yard in a purplish white light that reminded me of the parking lot at the high school. Pa came outside. "Bright as day out here, ain't it, Maggie? You could read a book. How about that."

The light attracted all kinds of bugs, and the nighthawks had a feast, flying themselves dizzy around the pole. I had collected a whole jarful of beetles by the time Stanley drove up.

"Damn!" Stanley said when he stepped out of the truck. "Where the hell did that come from?"

"Guess what, Stanley!" I yelled. "Pa bought a new yard light so we could join the twenty-first century. Mama hates it."

"This is a bad dream. It's like an operating room out here. Worse." Stanley stood in the center of the yard, looking up.

"You can't see the stars at all," I added.

"I know. We'll just have to figure out how to turn it off."

Then we discovered the worst thing about the yard light: you can't shut it off. Stanley simply didn't believe it.

"There's got to be a switch or something somewhere." He looked everywhere and even climbed partway up the pole. He finally said, "There are only two ways to shut it off. Cut the electrical supply to the whole place or shoot out the bulb."

I tried to get Stanley to watch the night-hawks catch moths in the unnatural lavender glow, but he refused. He ran down to the basement and began working furiously. I followed.

"The secret thing about the telescope," he told me, "is that we'll be able to look right past the stupid yard light like it isn't even there."

No criminals ever came, so Pa thought he was right to have gotten the light.

Stanley finished the telescope on August 16, 1962, my tenth birthday. Mama had kept me out of the kitchen all morning while she baked my birthday cake. When she finished it, she put it in the refrigerator so that the frosting wouldn't melt. Stanley had been working in the basement all day with the door locked.

It was getting dark when Pa finally got home. Mama had made my favorite supper—pork chops and applesauce—and set up the fan in the kitchen so that it would cool us while we ate. When everything was on the table, Mama called down the stairs to Stanley. We all sat down and waited.

"What the hell's he doing?" Pa said. "Get him up here." Mama called down into the basement again.

"In a minute!" Stanley yelled back.

"He's got nothing to do all day," Pa said, rising from his chair. "He can get his lazy butt up here to supper."

"I'll get him, Pa," I said quickly, running down the stairs. I met Stanley halfway and whispered, "Hurry! Pa's already mad." I could feel Pa's eyes on us when we sat down at the table.

"It's not too much trouble for you to come upstairs for your sister's birthday supper, I hope."

"I'm sorry I'm late, Pa. Sorry, Maggie. But I had to finish my project."

"You mean it's really finished?"

"Yes!"

"Hurray! On my birthday!" Stanley smiled.

"I'll show you all after dinner."

"I get to be first!"

"Yes, you do."

"Well, it's high time we get to see it!" Ma said, spooning applesauce onto her plate.

I sneaked a glance at Pa, but he seemed to have forgotten about the rest of us. He was absorbed in his eating, hunched over his plate, the cuffs of his shirt rolled up over his thin, sinewy forearms.

Then he announced, "Gary Gillis wants to rent our northeast section. Says he wants to keep his new machinery busy."

Mama held the plate of pork chops in midair for at least a minute.

"How much, Leo?"

"Fifty dollars an acre."

"Fifty! What did you tell him?"

"I told him no, of course. I farm my own land."

"Don't I have a say?"

"Pa," Stanley said quietly, "maybe you should take it a little easier."

Pa cut him short. "You know about taking it easy, don't you? Like I said, I farm my own land."

Mama passed the pork chops around for seconds. We ate silently, keeping a wary eye on Pa. I closed my eyes while Mama brought out the cake and lit the candles.

"Open your eyes and make a wish, Maggie. Hurry up before the candles drip."

The cake was beautiful—lemon-yellow frosting with loops of white icing down the sides.

"Well? Make a wish!" Stanley said.

"Come on, Maggie. The candles are already dripping."

At that moment I saw my family clearly for the first time. I saw Mama, smiling, and Pa down at the end of the table, still hunched over his plate but not eating. I saw Stanley's pale, handsome face across from me. Suddenly my wish seemed very important. I took a deep breath and held it. I decided not to waste the wish on Pegasus. I closed my eyes and wished the only wish that was clear in my mind—that Stanley would not be allergic to moondust—and I blew out all ten candles.

Mama and Stanley sang "Happy Birthday," and I felt my cheeks flush. I hated that part.

"Now, then," Mama said, after we'd eaten the cake and cleared the table, "let's see this big surprise, Stanley."

"Everybody has to go outside." He hesitated. "You too, Pa." Pa seemed to take no notice.

"Come on, Leo," Mama said. "Stanley wants us to go outside." Pa looked up at her like he was confused. "Come on. We're all going outside to see Stanley's project."

Stanley ran down the basement stairs two at a time, while the rest of us waited around in the backyard.

After a minute or two, Pa began saying, "What the hell's going on?"

Stanley emerged from the back door carrying a white-barreled telescope on an aluminum tripod. It was beautiful—just like the picture in *Scientific American.*

No one said anything at first. Stanley carried it to the middle of the yard and carefully spread the tripod legs, adjusted them, and locked them into place. He ran his hand along the smooth metal barrel and bent over the eyepiece to focus on the moon.

"Here, Maggie," he said. "The mountains of the moon." The telescope was gleaming. I was almost afraid to touch it. Then I drew in my breath and looked at another world.

"I see them, Stanley! You were right! The mountains, the craters, every single bit of the moon. Even some of the dark part."

Then Mama looked while I jumped up and down beside her.

"Well isn't this pretty!" Pa said to Stanley.

"It's a telescope, Pa," Stanley said cautiously. "I built it myself. Go ahead and give it a try."

"What would I want to do that for?"

Stanley's face tightened.

"Come on, Pa," Ma said. "It can't hurt to look." Pa bent over the eyepiece.

"I can't see a damn thing."

Stanley said, "You have to focus it, Pa. Turn this knob here until it looks clear." Pa fumbled with the knob. "Here, let me show you." Stanley turned the knob. "There. How's that?"

I held my breath. Pa looked for about ten seconds, then straightened up.

"Well, that's a pretty sight, Stanley. Looks like you did a fair job of building it, too." Pa slid his hands into his pockets and kicked at the dirt with the toe of his boot. "Trouble is, we don't need a damn telescope."

"Leo! What a thing to say! Stanley's been working on this telescope for weeks."

"That's what I'm talking about. Why can't he spend his time on something useful?"

"We can see the stars now, Pa, like we used to," I said. "We can't even see the Milky Way anymore since we got the yard light, and—"

"Well, that's fine," Pa interrupted. "Stargazing is fine for a little girl, but you'd think a boy of eighteen—a man in my day—would make himself useful. What good is a telescope to a farmer?"

"I'm not a farmer," Stanley said quietly.

"Excuse me, I forgot. Mister astronaut." Pa poked Stanley in the chest with his finger, then shoved him, not hard, but Stanley lost his balance and fell backward into the tripod legs. The telescope hit the ground with a sound that made me sick to my stomach. Stanley just lay there. For a moment Pa stood over Stanley and the telescope as if he were thinking what to do.

"It was an accident, Stanley," Mama said. "I know Pa didn't mean to do that, did you, Pa?" Pa extended his hand, but it was like Stanley couldn't see it. He was staring straight up into outer space, somewhere past Mars. Pa let his hand sink back to his side, then he shrugged.

"Then that's the end of that," he said, and headed back into the house.

"You okay, Son?" Mama asked.

Stanley hadn't moved since he hit the ground, but now he nodded and got to his feet slowly. His pants, the back of his shirt, and his hair were covered with dust. His breathing was bad. Mama put her hand on Stanley's shoulder.

"He didn't mean for that to happen. You know that."

"How do I know that, Ma?"

"He's your father. He's just trying to do the best he can with you kids—get you toughened up for life. And he's got problems of his own. You know how he is."

"Yeah," said Stanley. "I know."

"Don't take it personal," Mama hesitated. "If you're okay, I probably should keep an eye on Pa."

I watched Mama disappear into the light on the other side of the screen door. I could hear the television enough to recognize the program Pa was watching—*All-Star Wrestling*.

I knew Stanley didn't want me to look at him now. I tried to pick up the telescope and set it back on its legs, but the big mirror dropped out onto the ground. Stanley made no move to pick it up.

"You can fix it, Stanley. You made it." I shoved the glass disk into the end of the telescope. "Look, this is the only part that broke." I looked through the eyepiece into fuzzy grayness. "It's not too bad."

"Maggie, don't. You heard what Pa said. We're farmers. We don't need to see past the barn."

Stanley's pale skin looked ghostly in the purplish, buzzing glow of the yard light, and for the first time I felt afraid that Pa might be right, afraid that Stanley wasn't tough enough for life.

But I was wrong. About a week later, Stanley left the farm for college and never came back. He wrote from time to time, and I believe he was happy. Before he went, he fixed the telescope and left it on my bed.

His note said, "Keep an eye on the stars for me, kiddo."

I did what he asked. Every night that summer and every summer afterward, I took Stanley's white telescope down by the pond and watched the constellations spin across the sky, just beyond the barn.

The Kite Maker's Dream

by Jerry Daoust

Kiyoshi Morimoto's heart sank when he came puffing into the park behind his cart only to find young Jeremy Diggins once again thrown headfirst into the trash by his tormenter. He felt a deep sense of guilt at letting the boy down. Kiyoshi had promised to escort the eleven-year-old home from the park to keep the local bully from beating him up. It had been Kiyoshi's suggestion to find a peaceful alternative to Jeremy's idea for dealing with the bully, which was to get a weapon.

Now Kiyoshi was full of dread that the boy would be so frustrated, he would go ahead with that futile plan. Although it made him shudder to think of Jeremy with a knife—or worse, a gun—he could understand the boy's anger, his desire for the quickest way of making the bully stop. Kiyoshi might be sixty-six years old, but he still remembered his boyhood. Leaving his kite cart, the old man walked over to where Jeremy's feet kicked helplessly in the air. The boy was trying to push himself out of the container with his arms—an effort.

"Here I am," Kiyoshi said. "Please stop kicking, Mr. Diggins."

The boy's legs went limp. "Hurry," came the muffled plea from the bottom of the trash can. Kiyoshi tipped the container slightly and rolled it on its edge to a nearby park bench, where he leaned it at an angle. Although he was diminutive in stature and not as strong as he had been in his youth, he was able to pull the boy out, legs first, from his rude confinement.

Jeremy's reddish hair was matted down and full of crumbs of something; a wrapper stuck out of his orange sweatshirt. He sat down all sprawl-legged on the pavement, brushing himself off as he tried to stop crying, muttering angrily all the time about the boy who had deposited him in the trash in the first place. Kiyoshi brushed the boy off and then helped him up.

"Your ideas aren't working, Kiyoshi," the boy finally said. "Matt doesn't need love. He needs a punch in the nose, because he's just mean. I really hate him."

"You hate that he puts you in the trash," Kiyoshi said.

"No," Jeremy retorted. "I hate him. I hate his guts. I want to pound his face in until his brains leak out his ears."

"Jeremy," Kiyoshi said disapprovingly, but he didn't say anything more. He put his hand on the boy's shoulder and looked upon him sympathetically. Jeremy looked up at Kiyoshi's round face, which was shaped by kind lines, and colored a warm sort of brown. He pushed hard with his hands at the tears that ran down his face, as if wiping them away would wipe away his shame, too.

The clear sky was as bright as a blue porcelain bowl. "It's perfect kite-flying weather," Kiyoshi said.

They pushed the kite cart down a path that led to a fountain near a play area, where young parents rested on park benches as their children clambered around the climbing equipment. The side of the cart said, "Kiyoshi Morimoto's Fine Handcrafted Japanese Kites." The awning above the cart was painted with vivid pictures of the various kites for sale, many of which were on display in the cart's bamboo racks. Throughout the winter Kiyoshi worked in his shop making kites from *hachiku* bamboo and handmade paper on which he painted colorful designs with natural pigments. All summer long he sold the kites in the park. When they had first met last summer, Kiyoshi told Jeremy that although he did not make much money, he enjoyed his work, and that was more than could be said for many people in the city.

"I have a special kite for you today, Mr. Diggins," Kiyoshi said. "The *hinodetsuru,* the sunrise crane."

He removed it from the cart. It was a large kite made in the shape of a squatting crane that seemed to be laying eggs. A reddish orange crescent, the rising sun, peeped out from behind the crane's nest. "The crane is an auspicious symbol of a long, good life. The sunrise is for new beginnings."

"What's *auspicious?*" Jeremy asked.

"That means something good for you."

"It's pretty funny looking."

"Do you want to fly it or stand here criticizing the kite maker, hmm?"

The boy took the kite and let out the string until it caught on the breeze. The wind was just right, and the kite soared upward. Small children stopped playing and tilted their open-mouthed heads back to watch the kite. Jeremy balanced his gaze along the kite string, watching the crane rise gracefully ever higher. Kiyoshi had once explained that in Japan, kites are sometimes flown as prayers lifted up to the face of God. With this kite Kiyoshi offered Jeremy a prayer for the beginning of a good, rich life. A prayer for an end to his being picked on.

"Not too high," Kiyoshi said, eyeing the kite, which they could hear flapping briskly in the wind. "We want people to be able to see it. Preferably people with money to spend on a kite. . . . Maybe I should start flying these outside the windows of skyscrapers with rich yet oh-so-bored businesspeople inside. You think they would come out of their board meetings to fly a kite?"

"Yeah!" Jeremy said. "In school I'm always looking out the window watching for your kites."

"You should be paying attention in class," the kite maker murmured as he carefully brought a small flock of paper parrots from inside the cart. They were colored in brilliant reds, greens, and yellows, and all connected to one another with strings. When they flew on their outstretched wings, many passersby would mistake them for real birds—until they saw the string leading down to Kiyoshi's cart.

"Well, what should I do about Matt?" Jeremy said. "He won't leave me alone no matter what I do, and Mom says the police have better things to do than deal with boys' fights. Mom keeps on saying I've got to learn to stand up to him myself."

"You think you can beat him up?"

"No," Jeremy admitted ruefully. "But I'll bet he would stop if I could. Kyle takes a knife to school. If I had a knife."

"Didn't we already talk about why that's a bad idea?" Kiyoshi asked.

"I wouldn't use it, I would just scare him with it."

Kiyoshi shook his head. "Do you ever carry anything you don't intend to use? If you carry it, you will suddenly find yourself using it, or maybe it will be used against you."

"Okay, well, what am I supposed to do? You keep on saying not to fight him, but he keeps on picking on me and putting me in the trash. Should I buy a helmet so I don't get garbage in my hair?"

Kiyoshi smiled thinly. "No. We will find a way to make him stop bothering you, a way that is peaceful."

Jeremy rolled his eyes. "Yeah, that's what you keep saying."

"We must keep trying to find a peaceful way," Kiyoshi said slowly. "It's not easy, but I think together we are smart enough to do something clever that will persuade Matt to reconsider his behavior toward you. Peace is hard, violence is easy. Any animal can bite back against its opponent. That's blunt, and messy. But peace is an elegant thing, a beautiful thing, like a kite. You understand? To make anything as beautiful as a kite to fly requires intelligence, planning, and hard work. It is the civilized person who can make peace."

Jeremy stopped watching his kite to stare quizzically at Kiyoshi. "Man, were you like a hippie in the sixties or something? Because you sure seem big on all this peace stuff."

Kiyoshi began releasing the paper parrots out on the line one at a time so that they wouldn't get tangled with one another. "No," he said, "but I have seen war. You see, when I was your age, my older sister and my parents were killed by a nuclear bomb that was dropped on the city where we lived, Nagasaki."

Jeremy's eyes widened. "Serious? That would be scary."

"It was very scary," Kiyoshi said. "I had nightmares for many years."

The boy fell silent for a while. Some parents came and bought kites for their children, and Kiyoshi served them with one hand on the kite line and one hand changing money. When he was finished, he played out more line and brought the parrots as near as he dared to Jeremy's crane. The many parrots danced on the wind, their wings glowing in the sun like stained-glass windows. "Well, tell me what happened," Jeremy ventured after a while. "What was it like after they dropped the bomb?"

"Oh," Kiyoshi sighed, sorry he'd brought the subject up. "It's a long story."

"My mom isn't home until six, remember?"

Actually it wasn't the length of the story that had caused Kiyoshi to hesitate; it was the nature of it. He never liked remembering those things, and anytime he spoke of them, the memories rose up strong and vivid again in his mind.

"Still, there isn't enough time," Kiyoshi said. How could there ever be enough time, enough words, to re-create the power of that bomb? When he was younger, Kiyoshi had told the story to whomever would listen, hoping that if he did his hearers would be affected in the same way that he and all the children who survived the atomic bombs had been, so they would work for peace at all costs, and no other children would ever relive the horrors of war in a thousand nightmares. But no matter how he told his story, he never saw the light of full understanding in his listeners' eyes. Perhaps only the greenish white glare of the bomb, that burning light, could transform the hearts of those who saw it.

"I will tell you this much, Mr. Diggins," Kiyoshi said after a while, thinking that maybe the boy, being a child, would be able to hear his story in ways that others couldn't. "In the morning on the day the bomb fell, all was well with my world. I was only a child, you see; I hadn't really experienced the war. On that morning I ate bowls of rice with my gentle mother and my beautiful older sister, Hiroko. My sister took her lunch box and said to me, 'Good-bye, Yoshi-chan.' I left my mother and went to play in the river with my friends from the neighborhood. On my way to the river, I passed Sister Noguchi—who used to give us children sweets—working in the fields with the other Franciscan nuns, and they waved at me. I passed the grand Ura-kami Cathedral, where my family went to Mass every weekend. You see, many thousands of us in that district were Catholic. We were the largest Christian community in Japan.

"I went down to the river, where we boys always played a game called find the bell. We would throw a little silver bell into the river, and then dive in to see who could find it first. We were playing like that in the river when one of the boys pointed to the sky and said, 'Look, there's a B-29.' All the other boys looked, and while they were looking I threw the bell in the water and dove in after it, while they were distracted. When I was underwater, there was a tremendously bright flash, a flash of whitish green light. At first I thought it was the sun that had come out from behind the clouds, but it was far too bright to be the sun. It made my eyes hurt, even at the bottom of the river.

"When I broke the surface of the water, the air was roaring like a thousand jet engines, and it was so hot to breathe. My friends, all of them were dead, and there were no buildings left standing as far as I could see. Everything was like a black desert, charred by the heat. We never found my sister. My mother was burned to death under the rubble of our house. My father survived, but he died a few years later of leukemia, as so many did because of the radiation poisoning. The Urakami Cathedral was vaporized, along with all but one of the nuns, and the priests who said Mass there.

"The bomb destroyed the war factories and the soldiers' barracks, but it also killed almost a hundred thousand innocent people, including most of the Christians, old women, children, and animals. Thousands of children were orphaned, including myself. Among those of us who were orphaned, I know of none who did not become strong advocates of peace.

"So you see, Mr. Diggins, why I am opposed to fighting. It was fighting that stole my childhood world away from me. I think it causes great evil in the world."

The man and the boy were silent. The children laughed and called to one another, and the parents sat on park benches talking. The kites Kiyoshi flew had small metal whistles attached to them with string, and the whistles made flute like songs as the wind passed over them. Jeremy said nothing, and Kiyoshi was left to muse over the memories he had chosen not to share, memories from the three days he spent wandering Nagasaki in a daze, searching for his family.

All these years later, it seemed like such an awful nightmare. It was hard to believe the nightmare really happened. He remembered the face of the half-dead man, whose skin hung from his body like bloody rags, begging him for water to slake his burnt thirst. He remembered going to the river himself for water, only to find the surface covered with corpses gently floating and bumping into one another. He saw the face of a woman holding a bloody baby to her naked breast, both of them dead. And he remembered the boy he found crying for his mother. He and the boy spent the night under a tin lean-to by the river. They were so terrified by it all, yet too exhausted to panic anymore. They held on to each other tightly until they fell asleep under the orange, flame-filled sky.

Kiyoshi closed his eyes and willed the memories away, as he had so many times before. When he was younger, he had been convinced that he and all those who had passed through the power of that hell had been anointed prophets to warn the world of what lay in wait if it continued its wars. But it seemed to Kiyoshi that the world turned a deaf ear to the children who had walked out of the burning fire of the atomic bomb. If the world listened, it would know that in splitting open the atom, it had split open the gates of hell as well.

Jeremy said suddenly, "Do you think if I try to fight Matt, that's as bad as war?"

Kiyoshi regarded him thoughtfully. "No, that's not as bad as war," he said. "But small fights grow into big fights, which grow into wars. The fight between you and Matt is such a small thing. But so many small acts of violence add up, like drops of water add up to make a flood."

Jeremy scowled a bit. "Kiyoshi, did you have nightmares about the bomb?"

Kiyoshi nodded. "As a child I used to have nightmares of being bombed again, because to me it seemed as if the bomb had come out of the clear blue sky, with no cause. But the bomb that fell on me and my family didn't just suddenly appear out of nowhere, did it?"

"I know—it came from America," Jeremy said. "We studied it in school. They had a picture of the plane that dropped it."

"Yes, yes," Kiyoshi said slowly. "The bomb came from America, but why did America make the bomb? To stop the war, right? And the war came from many people acting out of fear and revenge and hate and a lust for power. And where did all those people learn these works of war? They learned them as children, you see." Kiyoshi paused and closed his eyes, wishing that this thin, red-haired, picked-on child might understand words spoken from an old man's heart. He opened his eyes and fixed them on Jeremy, pointing to the boy's own heart with a thin finger. "You have the power to stop war," he said.

"I can't stop war," Jeremy said. "I'm just a kid."

"It was just a little atom that killed one hundred thousand lives. If one small atom can unleash so much evil, how much more love, Mr. Diggins, do you think one small kid could bring into the world?"

They flew their kites for a while longer. Kiyoshi daydreamed about old Tokyo in the eighteenth century, when the whole city was so preoccupied with kite flying that even the merchants laid down their work to watch the skies. Before long Jeremy got bored and wanted to go play on the jungle gym with some other kids. He wound up the string until the crane kite rested in his hands. He held it up to the sun so that the light shone through the painting of the crane and the painted sun, making them glow as if they had come to life.

"You do good work making kites," Jeremy told Kiyoshi thoughtfully.

"Thank you," Kiyoshi said, tugging on his line to boost his parrots a little higher. Jeremy put the crane kite away in the cart.

"Will you teach me how to make kites?"

The sun was lower in the sky, and Kiyoshi squinted against it to see the boy clearly. "Sure," he said. "Sure, I can teach you that."

Kiyoshi's parrots remained in the sky, where the wind, like the breath of God, sustained them. And then Jeremy went off to play, which, Kiyoshi reflected, was just as it should be.

Filling the Shoebox

by Sara Lewis Holmes

Haley hadn't been inside many churches in her life, and never in a Catholic one, so she couldn't say if this one was normal. No stained glass. No pews. No arches. Just a large, beige-carpeted room with rows and rows of orange plastic chairs that linked together with metal hooks. A table covered with a plain, woven cloth stood on a raised platform at one end of the room. Behind it, on the wall, was a mosaic of shells and rocks that formed a cross. And everywhere else—under the chairs, and against the walls, and stacked in the corners—were piles and piles of cardboard shoeboxes.

"What do you think, Haley?" said her brother, throwing one arm around her shoulders. "Can you perform in such a lowly setting? Or does a dazzling comet like you need a bigger stage than Saint Mary's by the Sea?"

"This is fine," said Haley, straightening her new copper-tinted glasses, which Patrick had knocked askew. She felt sticky and tired after her drive from Durham, and she was sure her curly red hair was cometlike as usual. "Anything fancier and I'd get stage fright."

"No throwing up allowed," said Patrick. "I promised the fund-raising committee." He looked sideways at her, a playful expression on his plain, broad face. "Remember how you used to throw up before every show in high school?"

"Yup," said Haley. "And I guess I'll throw up before my court appearances, too, once I get through law school. But at least I'll be getting paid a lot more per upchuck." She grinned and tried not to think how many times she'd rehearsed that line. Rehearsed her reasons for choosing a life so different from Patrick's.

"Okay then," said Patrick as he took his arm off Haley's shoulder. "Mass starts at 5:30, so it'll be quiet in here for another hour if you want to look at the shoeboxes. I've got to polish my homily."

"Your what?" said Haley as he headed toward his tiny office.

"The sermon," said Patrick. "I'm not too good at them yet."

Sure, thought Haley, as she sank down into one of the orange plastic chairs. Like there's something you're not brilliant at. Patrick had always been the standard she measured herself by, the one to beat at school, at sports, at life in general. They'd compared batting averages in Little League, then SAT scores in high school, then GPAs in college. She'd always thought they'd compare salaries and number of kids too. Until Patrick dropped out of the astronomy and physics program at Chapel Hill. Converted to Catholicism. Became a priest.

I should have come to the ordination, she thought. Then maybe I'd understand some of this. But at the time, she'd been in the middle of exams, and it had seemed so easy to avoid the turmoil that Patrick's decision had caused in her family. So easy to avoid her own confusion and questions.

Now he worked here, at this strange church on North Carolina's Eastern Shore, this place that didn't even have the money for a paved parking lot. She'd come here this weekend because he'd asked her to be part of a talent show, a fund-raiser for the diocese's mission trip to Mexico next fall. But the real reason he'd wanted her to come was because of the shoeboxes.

"You're the one that gave me the idea for the project, Haley," he'd said on the phone. "Remember that time when I made fun of the humongous suitcase you always dragged to Granny's house in Knoxville for the summer? With all your books, and your hair stuff, and your clothes? And you told me you could fit everything you needed for three months into one shoebox?"

Haley remembered. She spent the whole summer washing the same pair of shorts over and over, and had cut her hair completely off rather than fight its unruly curls without a blow dryer. That was the summer Patrick had first teased her about being a comet.

"So anyway," Patrick had plowed on, not stopping for her reply, "I started thinking how much good stuff could fit in one shoebox. Toothbrushes, washcloths, razors, pencils and paper, small toys, that kind of thing. For the volunteers to distribute in Mexico."

Haley had to admit it was a good idea. She'd even said she would bring some donations herself when she came down. But then Patrick went on to say that he wanted her to write a play about the whole shoebox idea— for the youth to perform in churches up and down the beach this summer. To get people interested in supporting the shoebox project.

"Not a big, three-act play, Haley," he'd said. "Just a one-act. Something about shoeboxes, living simply, sharing what you have. You could even use the shoeboxes as part of the play itself, as props or scenery or something."

She had told him no. Not even a chance.

"I can't write a play this summer, Patrick. I've got articles to finish for the *Law Review,* and my clerking job is really overwhelming right now, and besides that, I don't . . . well, I don't know much about . . . God and all that stuff."

"You don't have to write about God," Patrick had said. "Just shoeboxes. At least come and see them, and then you can decide."

Haley looked at the piles of shoeboxes all around her. Where had they all come from? A lot of them still had price stickers. One hundred and fifty dollars for a pair of kids' basketball shoes. Eighty dollars for a pair of high heels. There were even several large boxes stamped U.S. Army that must have contained boots for soldiers. From Fort Bragg, probably.

Haley opened one of the boxes. In it was a blue terrycloth towel, a small bottle of shampoo, a package of yellow number two pencils, some gum, and a child's jump rope. A handwritten note read: *"Hasta la vista,* baby. Love, Samantha, age eight." Haley laughed. Those were probably the only Spanish words Samantha knew. But the picture under the words was better. A drawing of a little girl, running, with a shoebox balanced on her head, from North Carolina all the way, on a purple dotted line, to Mexico.

Haley opened another box. It was empty, as was the next one she checked, and the next. Maybe the fund-raiser tonight would help fill these boxes. Maybe Patrick wouldn't need her play after all.

An hour later, after she'd taken a shower and changed into a skirt, she was back in the church, in one of the same uncomfortable chairs. This time she was surrounded by other people—families, old folks, teenagers. Some of them wore nice clothes like her, but some, smelling of suntan lotion and sporting sunburned faces, wore shorts. Tourists, Haley guessed. That's how I feel in this place. Like a tourist, she thought. Especially when everybody around her seemed to know what they were doing, standing up and sitting down at the appropriate times, saying lines from memory, and generally looking comfortable with the whole idea of Patrick, her brother, as a priest.

"Consider the lilies, how they grow," Patrick read as the people stood and listened. "They neither toil nor spin; but I tell you, even Solomon in all his glory did not clothe himself like one of these. But if God so arrays the grass in the field, which is alive today and tomorrow is thrown into the furnace, how much more will He clothe you, O men of little faith! And do not seek what you shall eat, and what you shall drink, and do not keep worrying."

Does Patrick really believe what he's reading? thought Haley. That you could trust God that much? Patrick seemed so sure of his faith, of his chosen path, and she . . . she didn't even know if she'd made the right choice in pursuing law school. Some days even the thought of the big money she would eventually make didn't help her get through the day-to-day grind of classes. But she didn't dare back out now, especially with student loans to pay off and her plans to buy a new car when she graduated.

"For all these things the nations of the world eagerly seek," Patrick read on, "but your Father knows that you need these things. But seek for His Kingdom, and these things shall be added to you." He raised the book above his head. "This is the Word of the Lord."

"Praise to You, Lord Jesus Christ," the people around Haley said, then sat down, leaving her standing alone for a split second before she realized her error. Blushing, she sat down quickly, her feet bumping against the shoebox stashed under her chair.

Then Patrick gave his homily, a short talk about the mission project and how it related to the passage he'd just read. Haley listened intently, hoping for some insight into what he might want from her play, but she couldn't connect with his words. Yes, she understood how living more simply might be a good thing. Wouldn't her own life be a lot easier if she didn't have to worry about her car that kept breaking down, her apartment that needed constant straightening, her clothes that had to be dry cleaned? But how could anyone really live simply when the world was so complicated?

Haley turned this question over and over in her mind as the Mass continued, until finally, the people began rising by rows and going forward to take Communion. Haley felt awkward and alone, staying seated as the others rose around her. So when her row went forward, she reached for the shoebox under her chair and, holding it to her chest, she slipped out of the church.

The air outside was still, and Haley could smell the slightly sour smell of a beach town. Closer to the water, the air would be fresher, and the rush of the waves, peaceful. But here, in the gravel parking lot, she could hear only the traffic from the coast road and the harsh cries of the foraging seagulls. Haley sat on one of the stumpy, treated-timber posts that marked out the parking lot, and put the shoebox on the ground at her feet.

What exactly had she packed in her box that summer? What had been important to her when there wasn't room for anything but the essentials? She couldn't remember anything but the warm laughter of her grandmother when she'd showed up without the usual exploding suitcase. Now she hardly ever saw Granny. There never seemed to be time, or money, for a visit.

Haley dug in her purse for her keys and went to her faded green compact car. In the passenger seat were a pad of yellow legal paper and a pencil. She took them both back to the post she had been sitting on and sat there, staring at the shoebox at her feet. She began to make a list. A list of what she thought had been in the box that summer. Her favorite shorts. Two T-shirts. Probably her tape player and tapes. The lip gloss her mother had recently let her start wearing. A book? A stuffed animal—had she still been sleeping with them? Her best friend's address so that they could write to each other all summer. Her swimming suit. The letter that Granny had sent, detailing all her plans for the three of them that summer. At the bottom, she'd written, "We're going to have fun. Trust me."

And I did trust her, thought Haley. Or else I never could have left my suitcase behind.

"Haley?" called a voice. Patrick. The Mass must be over. "You're not throwing up out here, are you?"

Haley smiled. "No," she responded, as he crunched across the parking lot, still in his long robes. "Just thinking. Thinking about what was in my box that summer. How little I really needed because I knew Granny would take care of me, no matter what."

Patrick nodded. "Sounds like a good idea for a play. What do you think?"

Haley picked up the shoebox from her feet and took a deep breath. Now was the time to tell him that he should give up on her and this play. That she wasn't the same girl who had impulsively answered his challenge that summer. That she didn't know God like he did, and that she just couldn't fit her life into a shoebox anymore.

"I don't know if I can trust God the way you do, Patrick," she began. "All that stuff about 'not worrying, and all these things being added unto you' seems pretty radical to me. But I want . . ." She stopped as a sudden rush of stage fright rumbled in her stomach. What did she want? The shoebox was so light in her hands that she felt it might rise into the air like one of the gulls. I want to know why you became a priest, she thought. I want to call Granny and see how she's doing. I want to feel less like a tourist in church, and more like I belong, the same way I felt that summer, connected to and cared for by the people I loved.

It was too much to want, all at once, so instead she simply said to Patrick, as if it were the easiest thing in the world, "I want to try to write the play."

They walked back to the church together, Patrick's arm around her shoulders, and her glasses once again slightly askew. The shoe-box Haley carried was still as light as air, but she held it firmly, as if it contained everything she needed for the summer.

Loaves and Fishes

by Sara Lewis Holmes

Three black iron fishes and a loaf of bread, all of them spotted with rust, were bolted to the outside wall of the soup kitchen. Above them a hand-lettered white sign read: "Lunch served daily: 11:30–1:00."

It was a perfect shot, thought Lia, but the shadow cast by the overhanging eaves was going to make exposing it tricky. She closed in a step, cradling her camera and concentrating on the picture. Her short red hair was tucked behind her ears, tinged with sweat from the hot-already Georgia sun. A worn camera case stuffed with rolls of film, assorted lenses, and her flash hung from one shoulder. She was eighteen but looked even younger in her wrinkled shorts and T-shirt, drawn straight from the pile of clean laundry she'd never bothered to fold.

"Thank the Lord. Someone's here," said a voice.

Lia drew her eye away from the camera, blinking as the world enlarged again outside the frame of the lens. A tall, brown-skinned woman in a tan business suit stood in the open door of the soup kitchen. She had a crisply made-up face, and a cropped angular haircut. Around her waist was a green apron with an image of a loaf of bread and a cross stamped on it.

"I'm sorry," said Lia. "I should've asked before I started taking pictures. Is it okay? I'll be out here about twenty minutes. Then I'd like to come inside and shoot there, too, if you don't mind."

The woman laughed in short warm bursts.

"Honey, I'm a volunteer. As far as I know, you can take all the pictures you want. But first, you can help me serve food. The man who was supposed to come called and his car won't start, and I can't feed three hundred people by myself."

Lia almost lost her voice for a second.

"I'm not sure I can," she managed to say. "I'm on a deadline."

But the woman had already taken Lia's arm and steered her inside.

"You don't look old enough to be on the city paper," she said. "Are you with the University one?" She slipped a green apron over Lia's head and tied it firmly in the back. "And what's your name?"

"Lia. I'm not at the U. Maybe next year, if I get the money," said Lia, her mind turning as she talked. How am I going to tell this woman that I don't have time to help her?

"I'm doing a photo essay for my boyfriend's 'zine. He started it last year. He's a journalism major."

"So was I," said the woman. "That was before psychology and after pre-law. Now I'm in banking." She led Lia through a maze of Formica-topped tables. They were set with cardboard salt and pepper shakers and neat stacks of brown paper towels. "By the by, my name's Marion, and we're serving chicken and biscuits today. Anthony's got it mostly ready, but we'll have to carry it out to the warming trays in about ten minutes. I'll put your camera on that high shelf over there. It'll stay out of the food that way."

Lia grabbed for her camera strap, but Marion had already whisked it away.

"Don't worry, sweetheart," said Marion. "The other volunteer is trying to get a ride over here with his neighbor. You probably won't have to serve but half an hour; then you can snap away."

Lia sighed. Marion had a lot in common with a steamroller. She handed Marion her camera bag too.

"A half an hour. But I have to use the phone first."

She'd told Zach she would meet him in an hour at the student union so they could have coffee and lunch together before he drove home for spring break. And so she could give him the film. Usually she developed her own film, but Zach wanted all the materials for the next issue early, so that he could work on the 'zine over the break. That was just like him, not to compromise his standards.

The phone was in the back, down a short dark hallway near the kitchen. An enormous man with a full beard and tattooed arms was squeezed into the tiniest cooking space Lia had ever seen. He was pulling a pan of flour-dusted biscuits from an ancient-looking oven. Must be Anthony, thought Lia as she dialed Zach's number. He'll make a great picture, if I can figure out how to get myself in there with him to get the shot.

Zach didn't answer. She left a message saying she'd be late, and hoped he would check his machine before he headed out to meet her. She didn't want to fight with him right before he left town for ten days. They had been fighting a lot lately. Last week he'd started in on why she couldn't help him with the 'zine on Sunday mornings instead of going to Mass with her family.

"Church is a luxury, Lia," he'd said, with his usual fierce honesty. "What good does all your kneeling and singing and blessing bread do if there are people eating sandwich crusts out of trash cans?"

Lia didn't know how to answer him, except to say that the images of the Mass, the

words and the shapes, filled her up somehow, like taking photographs did. Zach didn't
understand, but then he was always looking
at the big picture, thinking about long-term
solutions, and challenging others, through his
'zine, to do the same. Lia tended to focus on
the details of life, the one broken button on
a man's collar, the juice stain on a child's
mouth, the light falling on water. She hoped
this photo essay might convince Zach that
she cared about the big issues, too.

"Five minutes!" called Marion as she came
down the hall. "They're lining up outside.
Let's get this food out front." She took a large
tray of chicken pieces from Anthony and tilted her head toward Lia. "Anthony, this is
who the Lord sent us today. Her name's Lia.
Give her that load of green beans."

Anthony winked at Lia as Marion marched
down the hall.

"She's the boss of a big bank downtown.
Comes here on her lunch hour two days a
month and sets us straight."

Lia smiled and took the beans, maneuver-
ing them around the boxes stacked in the
hallway. She poured them into one of the
warming trays out front. Marion had opened
an industrial-sized can of fruit cocktail and
was spooning it into a serving dish.

"Anthony, deliver those biscuits!" she called
back to the kitchen. "I'm going to open the
door!"

When the door opened, an orderly crowd of men filed in. Lia saw that many of them were in work clothes, the muddy overalls of a construction crew, or the oil-stained striped shirts of a car repair place. There were women, too, some pregnant, a few with little kids on their hips, and some followed by older boys and girls that Lia was sure ought to be in school. Nearly all of them were black, which Lia guessed was because of the part of town they were in. The part her father always told her to stay away from.

"Don't forget to sign in," announced Marion, steering the line toward a faded green ledger book. "We need to know how many we're feeding." She came back behind the counter and handed Lia a plastic plate. "You put on the chicken, a little gravy, and a biscuit; I'll do the green beans and fruit. They get their own forks and drinks."

Lia got the hang of the system quickly, but it was hard to concentrate on the plates when her eyes kept framing pictures she'd like to take. There was the woman with the toddler on her back—the child was eating a saltine cracker and raining crumbs into his mother's cornrowed hair. The scrawny white man with the rheumy eyes and a faded bandanna tucked around his neck. The twin brothers, elbowing each other as they dug through the pile of donated books in the far corner. The line of people itself, curving gently from the door, shuffling toward her in a slow dance that seemed familiar to Lia, although she couldn't say why.

"Marion, we've got a problem," said Anthony, looming over Lia and startling her from the rhythm of the plate filling. He smelled of stale cigarettes and fresh soap. "The oven's broke again." Marion snorted.

"Of course. It's due. Did you get the next batch of chicken cooked or are we up a creek?"

Anthony pulled at one of his ears.

"There's always that ham place. If you run over there and get some of their extras, we can do ham biscuits until I beat some sense into that oven."

Marion was already taking off her apron.

"I'm out the door. Hold down the fort, Lia, honey. Go easy on the chicken."

Wait a minute, Lia wanted to say. What about my pictures? What about Zach? You can't drag me in here and then leave me on my own. I didn't sign up for this! But before she could find her voice, Marion was gone, the screen door banging behind her.

"Call me if you need me," said Anthony, patting her shoulder, "but yell loud, because I'll be under the old black beast."

"What if I run out of food?" said Lia, keeping her voice low so that the people waiting wouldn't hear. Anthony shook his head at her.

"Never have. Remember them loaves and fishes out front." He lumbered down the hallway.

Lia stared at the food in front of her. Her stomach cramped. She was starting to get hungry herself, since she'd skipped breakfast. There were lots of biscuits, and a decent amount of green beans, but the chicken pan was half-empty. There were probably fifteen to twenty pieces. The line was still to the door. Loaves and fishes! How could Anthony say that? She wasn't Jesus, to make food multiply out of thin air.

She looked at the people sitting at the long tables, eating, some in silence, some chatting and laughing between bites. No one stayed long, and everyone wiped their place after they stood up. She knew what Zach would say about them.

"They need better-paying jobs, Lia. That's the long-term answer." And she knew it was, too. But they are getting to eat today, she thought. And they aren't alone.

She looked back at the dwindling food. Maybe she could break the remaining pieces of chicken into the gravy and spoon them over a biscuit split in half. She quickly tore the chicken into bite-sized pieces and stirred

them into the thick, oatmeal-colored gravy.
At least there were plenty of biscuits.

Lia filled a plate with her makeshift casse-
role and handed it to the next person in line.
Reached for another plate and filled it too.
Go slow, she thought. Maybe that other man
whose car was broken would show up. Or
maybe Zach would get her message and
come looking for her. Make the food last,
she prayed. Make it last until Marion gets
back.

"You're new, ain't you?" said a gravelly
voice. A damp hand grabbed her wrist.

Lia looked up to see that one of the men
had reached across the counter. He was
dressed neatly, in a worn black pair of pants
and a faded blue shirt, but he was sweating
profusely, and his eyes were streaked with
red. His unshaved upper lip twitched as he
talked.

"You've got real pretty hair," he said, leaning toward her. "Real pretty."

Lia twisted her hand away from him. She
saw that his pupils were dilated.

He's high, she thought as she broke open
a biscuit. Really high. Act like you don't hear
him. Fix his plate. He'll move on.

"What's the matter? Don't you want to talk
to me?" said the man.

Lia's cheeks felt hot. She stared at the two white round biscuits, pretending she was looking through the lens of her camera, framing the shot. Too much white on white. She'd have to shoot the biscuits against a darker background if she wanted to capture their texture and perfect plain shape.

"I think I like you," said the man, louder now.

Lia ladled the chicken over the biscuit, then added some beans and fruit. Keep working. Stay calm. Don't answer him.

She held out the full plate. "Here's your food," she said.

The man didn't take the plate. He stared at her, his lips opening and closing with a wet popping sound. Lia felt her hands shaking. Should she call for Anthony? Would he hear her?

The next person in line, a gangly boy about Lia's age, gave the drugged man a slight shove.

"Didn't you hear the girl?" he said. "Take it and eat."

For this is my body, came the words leaping into Lia's head. She took the man's hands and placed them around the plate. His hands were shaking, too, but he held on to it. After a minute he drifted to a seat near the door. Lia inserted her thumbs into the next biscuit and broke it. This is my body, given for you.

Fifteen minutes later, Marion was back, bearing a tray of ham, and towing another woman behind her.

"I stopped off and grabbed my sister. She's always good in an emergency." Marion admired Lia's makeshift chicken dish, then gestured to the shelf. "Go on, honey. Don't you have some pictures you need to be taking?"

Lia retrieved her camera, then stepped around the counter and slipped through the tables to the far end of the room. First, the big picture, a shot of the gently swaying line streaming up to the table to be fed. Later, when she got to the close-ups, she'd have to figure out a way to photograph biscuits.

Going Home

by Lenore Franzen

The only memories Lucy could still touch were faded, like old photographs. They were of a life so different from hers now, of a time so far removed, that she often wondered, while feeding the pigeons on the Mall, why these scenes from the past persisted. Did they belong to her? Or had she acquired them from some unknown source, like the odd layers of clothing that hung loosely on her frail body?

She fumbled in her pocket for what she'd saved from the soup kitchen. Her fingers closed around a hard roll. She pulled it out, furtively glancing to see if anyone noticed. A few figures hurried down the path or across the lawn, but no one was looking at her. Her hand relaxed. Her eyes closed, and she recalled the doughy fragrance of the Christmas bread she used to make. And with the bread came the bitterness of cardamom, the richness of almond she used in her holiday baking.

Advent had been their favorite time of year. Even with her parents gone and Bill's parents too sick to travel, they had shaped a fullness around the carols, the activities, the waiting. Especially when their son was born. Lucy helped with the children's program, Bill sang in the choir. On Christmas Eve they came home to their small apartment, filled with the aromas from the oven, the balsam tree in the corner, and the boughs Lucy arranged as a centerpiece.

The memory of these smells reached all the way to the pit of her stomach. These images, so colored with detail, must be hers, she decided, opening her eyes. Yet claiming them didn't ease the gnawing inside. She had eaten, but when? Yesterday? How long had the roll been in her coat? She shook off the questions, knowing she had no answers. Instead, her fingers tore at the crust. She put her hand down, palm open, and made a low, guttural noise in her throat, like the purr Dolce, her cat, used to make when Lucy rubbed her ears. Before long the pigeons approached, bobbing their heads in a persistent yes, speaking a language that she found strangely comforting. They were, after all, her companions most days. Lucy felt their sharp, beady eyes stare at her intently and wondered what they saw. Did they see a woman whose mind played tricks on her? Did they know she was once too busy to sit on a bench all day and feed the birds? Did they see a woman who had been loved, even when she had been too lost to love back?

Lucy grew wary of this woman who seemed so strangely familiar. She avoided storefronts—all things glass—especially on bright days, because of the reflection thrown back at her. It frightened Lucy when she caught a glimpse of the figure. Her heart pounded furiously, and she looked away before the woman's piercing eyes shattered her shell. She also walked at some distance from the Reflecting Pool, not wanting to come too close to what those dark waters might reveal.

Water. Where else was there water? The question caught her off guard, and she shifted on the bench. Water. Her arm went limp. She let the rest of the crumbs fall from her hand, oblivious to the racket the pigeons made fighting over the sudden feast. She had run the water long and hot the night Bill left. She remembered how, afterward, her skin was pink and tingly, like a newborn's, and how light she felt. Her son was still there. He'd take care of her.

Bill had tried to hold the family together after he was laid off in Chicago. He had taken odd jobs here and there, but nothing ever lasted, and the bills kept piling up. Lucy pulled her coat around her to stop the memory, but it kept coming. She had tried to be encouraging, assuring him as much as herself that everything was going to be all right. She had tried to make do with less. She had pleaded with the landlord to let them stay through July, then August, sure that by then her husband would have a paycheck. She had even sold her wedding ring to buy their son clothes for school. When the look of defeat on Bill's face became a permanent mask, she could bear it no longer. It was his fault that her life was falling apart. His fault that they were going to starve. Soon she let words she meant to keep to herself slip. Good for nothing. Loser. Some provider you are. She stopped going to church, afraid to meet the looks of the other women whose husbands were still employed.

She took to locking herself in the bedroom for hours at a time, curled up in a ball, her eyes shut tightly against her shrinking world. She sought that familiar tunnel with endless passageways, each one leading her further down and away from the light.

When Lucy was in grade school, her mother had tried to protect her from the tunnel. "If you're feeling down, you just have to will yourself out of it," her mother had told her more than once. "That's what my mother did, and what I've always done." Her mother had insisted on the name Lucy, which meant "light," and pretended, as if it were some childhood game, that the dark monster simply didn't exist.

But Lucy felt its heavy breath on her many times. At night it entered her room and sat near her, on her bed. She lay there, unable to cry out, unable to tell it to leave. Soon she grew used to its presence, like a constant shadow, looking for it even on a cloudy day. And so she had grown up with one persistent companion. When she met Bill at church and they began dating, her mother had been triumphant. "Now you'll have children and be happy," she had said. "You'll have someone to take care of you and protect you."

Lucy and Bill had married and had a son, even though her pregnancy nearly killed her. Her doctor warned her against having more children. "The risk is too great," he had said. Bill was crushed, but Lucy merely relieved. One spirited child was proving quite enough for her to handle.

As for happiness, Lucy couldn't remember if it had ever been part of her life's equation. She wasn't even sure what it was. She caught glimpses of it in others; sensed, briefly, a tingling joy inside when she felt movement in her womb. But the notion of happiness seemed so ephemeral, so elusive, not something one possessed for any length of time.

Lucy had watched their son grow. Learn to walk, talk, run, play, explore. She felt a warm tug deep within whenever she saw him, yet she always felt a distance she couldn't quite close. She never mentioned this to Bill, or anyone. Her feelings, like the monster, were her secret.

After Bill had gone, Lucy spent more and more time locked in the bedroom. Her son was off playing with friends, no doubt, or watching TV. One day she heard a soft scrape on the floor. She forced her eyes open and saw an envelope slide under the door. She read it. Her son's draft notice. Number 16. The same as the date of his birthday. She hugged herself as tears streamed down her face. She sensed her son, standing beyond the locked door, waiting for her to come to him, to break the silence. Dear God, when he's gone, who will take care of me? He was her last hope, yet she did nothing.

Here Lucy's memory began to break down. She recalled someone screaming, and the neighbors pounding on the walls. Had there been another voice, his, perhaps, pleading with her to stop? To come out? That memory, each time it surfaced, teased her with the same question. Had her son left before she could say good-bye?

She didn't remember leaving the bedroom, but she would never forget being asked questions and more questions by the man at the hospital. He had told her matter-of-factly that she had had a nervous breakdown, that her family had a history of melancholy. She had pulled her hair until a clump came out, her eyes welling. Why hadn't anyone told her this before? Didn't the man know it was too late? Her husband and her son were already gone.

Lucy blinked as the late afternoon sun pierced through the trees. Abruptly she stood, then reached out to steady herself. The crumbs caught in her lap fell to the ground, but she wasn't thinking of bread or pigeons. In the quiet passages of her head, Lucy heard a far-off child's voice calling to her. Mother! Mother! The sound drew her along the path. She hurried as best she could on the crushed rock, her legs stiff from sitting so long. She stumbled twice, trying to reach the voice that stayed just ahead of her on the breeze. She wished she could go faster, but her shoes felt like weights, dragging her back with each step.

Her eyes darted left and right, scanning the trees, the monuments, the vast expanse of green. Her pulse quickened. Where was the child who so desperately needed her? A dizziness seized her and she stood very still, waiting for the trees to stop spinning. When they did, her eyes focused on a long gleaming wall made of the blackest stone.

Now the voice was closer, as if the person speaking were right beside her. Mother! it pleaded. Forgive us. Dad and I didn't know what to do when you were sick. She extended her arm to touch the tender voice, hoping, finally, to close the distance she had kept between them. Forgive you? What did you do? It is me that needs forgiving. She took a step closer, still avoiding her reflection in the stone. A chill ran up her arm when she touched the cold, smooth granite. Her fingers found the name, near the wall's center, six rows down, and traced each chiseled letter: *J-E-F-F-R-E-Y L-I-N-D-B-E-R-G*. For this she had come to Washington. The wall had been there when she walked this way before, yet she couldn't recall ever hearing Jeffrey speak to her until now. Had she been too far into the tunnel?

Her only son. Gone like her husband into some distant darkness she could never quite reach. Each night she laid their memories beside her, one on each side, protecting them while she slept.

Twilight spilled the wall's angular shadow over her feet, bathing them in its coolness. Lucy straightened her shoulders, shook off her weariness. Today Jeffrey had spoken to her. She turned and began to walk.

She wouldn't go to the shelter tonight. Too many faces, too many smells, too many children. Last time she had watched a mother trying to calm her fretful boy. She wanted to say, I know how to do that. I used to stroke my son's back when he fought bedtime. I

used to whisper songs in his delicate ear:
Jesus loves you this I know, for the Bible
tells me so. . . . But then she had caught
herself just in time. If she spoke of the past
out loud, the memories would become too
real, and she would experience the anguish
and loss all over again.

The exhausted mother had stared at Lucy
with vacant eyes. Lucy had clapped her hand
to her mouth. She recognized the mother's
expression as one she had worn in the hospital. Am I that empty, too? A shiver had run
through Lucy, and she had buried her face in
the hard pillow. She began to rock back and
forth, as she had rocked Jeffrey, mumbling,
Now I lay me down to sleep, I pray the Lord
my soul to keep. If I should die before I
wake, I pray the Lord my soul to take.

No more shelters, thought Lucy, her step as
firm as her decision. Night blanketed the city,
muting the day's harsher sounds. Car lights
and streetlights merged into a glowing halo.
A strange calmness settled over her. She forgot her hunger, her exhaustion. Even her
memories faded. She kept walking. Her feet
seemed to be taking her somewhere, and she
didn't resist.

Lucy licked her dry lips when she saw the
water fountain. Bending to it, she held the
cool liquid in her mouth, shivering at its
pureness. Then, in gulps, she drank deeply

from the stream, wiping her mouth with the back of her hand. She was about to splash some water on her face but heard footsteps nearby. Then she shrugged. What did they have to do with her? She had been in the tunnel long enough to know she was the only one there, and had been for some time.

Her feet guided her past the Botanic Gardens, and she followed. Several blocks off the Mall was a church. One window on the side was lit from within. She moved toward the glow, instinctively. The neighborhood was unfamiliar, quiet. Lucy peered up at the stained glass. It was dirty with soot, but she could just make out the figure—a man on a cross.

Her son, and the rest of his platoon, in Vietnam just a week, had burned alive when their transport plane was shot down, the telegram had said. Jesus. Jeffrey. The two names whirled in her head, spinning a web around her and holding her fast. Both suffered so much for her sake, and both forgave her. The litany rose to her lips. Have mercy on me.

She touched her chest. It was still there, where she always had it pinned to her dress. When her first life had ended, she hadn't known how strong the memories would be, which ones would linger or haunt her, so she chose one piece from her past, the letter

Jeffrey had sent when he first arrived for active duty. She hadn't read it for—how long? Time was a blur, for which Lucy was grateful. If she had been able to distinguish days from weeks from years, she would see how empty they were.

She reached down the neck of her sweater and unpinned the letter. Her fingers shook as she unfolded the damp paper. She smiled when she heard footsteps approaching. . . . Why, of course, Jeffrey's coming. . . . The letter was more than a memory; he was coming to her. She glanced up at the window and gave thanks.

Lucy savored her forgiveness like a rich chocolate. I have been forgiven all this time and only today did I taste its sweetness, she thought, as something heavy crushed her skull. Her legs gave way and she fell to her knees. Another blow, this time to her neck, and a gurgling moan spilled from her throat. From a great distance, she saw her hand rise up to touch the light in the window. Or was it a star?

Lucy lay crumpled on the sidewalk in a spreading stillness. The night met her, its cool breath blowing out the fire burning inside. She no longer fought for air. The darkness that had been with her for so long was now a brilliant weightlessness. And of her suffering, what did it matter? Even as her eyes emptied, she saw the door she would enter. I'm going home.

El Milagro

by Carol Estes

It's winter. Late afternoon. Real quiet. My best friend, Henry, and me, we're standing in the market square in Santa Fe, waiting for the bus, dancing around, blowing on our fingers to keep from freezing. It's been snowing all day long, off and on, so the Sunday tourist buses didn't show. Usually there's a row of Indians leaning against the building there, with blankets up over their heads like hoods, selling their silver jewelry. But most of them have already left. The rest are packing up. The smell of corn tortillas and green chilis from the cantina down the street is making me and Henry crazy.

Suddenly this beam of sunlight flashes through the clouds and hits the square so hard it shatters into a million pieces like shrapnel. One poor guy happens to be walking across the square. It stops him in his tracks, like a flashbulb, or a strobe light. He's x-rayed, outlined in light, fire in the ends of his hair and fingers.

That's it. It's over.

"Holy smokes!" I'm yelling. "What was that?"

Henry is looking paralyzed, like a deer caught in the headlights.

I check out the guy who nearly got fried. He keeps on walking like nothing happened. I check out the other people in the square to see if anybody's standing around looking amazed or staring at a hole in the sky with doves coming out of it or anything.

Nothing. People go on about their business, calm as you please.

"Man! Some kind of atmospheric thing," I say.

Henry's still saying nothing, but he has started looking kind of holy. "Maybe it's a sign," he says.

I get nervous when people go religious on me. So right away I start joking around about "the Incident." I get the idea to call it El Milagro, which, I inform Henry, means "miracle" in Spanish. I keep saying "El Milagro" over and over in a deep announcer voice. But Henry is not laughing.

"We've got ourselves an angel or a saint or something," says Henry. "Stranger things have happened, Leon," he says.

I snort—a habit I picked up from my old man. "Probably just one of those optical illusions. Like a sun dog or Saint Elmo's fire or something." I'm a year older than Henry, even though we're in the same class in school, so when I say things that have to do with life experience, he usually listens. But not this time. "You must have been looking at something else, then," he says, even though he knows it's a lie.

So I scope out the scene again, and its looking real ordinary. I'm starting not to believe my own eyes. "Freak nature things happen all the time," I say, "like two-headed calves, or frogs frozen in hailstones. . . ."

"Shut up!" Henry whispers. The man is coming right over to us. Henry and I look at each other. Turns out the guy is a friend of ours. Sort of. His name is Esteban—or so he says. He's got a week-old beard and greasy hair like half the men who sleep in doorways around here, and a paper bag is sticking out of his pocket, twisted tight around the neck of a bottle.

"There's your angel," I whisper to Henry. I think about crossing the street, since Esteban is the type who will hit us up for some change, but I know Henry won't do it. So we stand there. Esteban passes right by without even seeing us, leaving behind the smell of piss and booze. So I'm sniffing the air. "Shocking!" I say. "These angels today!"

Henry pays no attention. He's still standing around smiling like a stone saint or something, watching Esteban head down the block and around the corner. Then suddenly he takes off running after Esteban.

I catch up with Henry outside the Loretto Chapel, one of the local tourist attractions. "C'mon, Leon! He's in there," Henry says. He's excited, like this should be proof of something.

Truth is, the Loretto Chapel is not one of my favorite places. I don't come here much anymore. My old man was always dragging me and my little brother down here to show us the stairs Saint Joseph built. Then he'd make us go to confession. But I follow Henry and Esteban inside, just in time to see Esteban walk right past the girl at the desk and right past the box where you're supposed to put your donation. She opens her mouth to say something but takes one look at Esteban and decides to forget it.

The old tape recording about the church is playing over the loudspeaker, the part where the announcer asks you to put your money in the box for the Sisters of Loretto retirement fund. The machine stops, clunks a couple times, and starts over. A deep voice says, "Welcome to Loretto Chapel." It tells how the chapel was built by some pioneer nuns about a hundred years ago, and how you can rent it out for weddings and funerals or whatever. It even has a gift shop with everything you'd never want, like tapes of nuns singing and a bunch of history books.

Naturally Esteban could care less about this stuff. He doesn't even glance at the plaster altar painted to look like marble. He doesn't look at the stained-glass windows brought over from Italy. He just clumps along in his army boots on the stone floor, making a big hollow sound.

Nobody's left in the chapel except one pair of yuppie *turistas,* down in front by the postcards. They spot Esteban. "Well, honey," says the guy, looking at his Rolex. "Time to get going."

"If Esteban's going to confession," I whisper to Henry, "we're gonna be here all night."

"Shut up," Henry says.

Esteban heads right for the world-famous miracle stairs.

I once did an extra-credit, five-page paper for Sister Celestine on this very set of miraculous stairs, and I didn't have to look up a thing. My old man had told me the story a hundred times. Seems this big-shot architect from France built the choir loft twenty-five feet in the air but forgot the stairs. No problem, he says to the nuns, you can use a ladder. But not even pioneer nuns are going to climb a ladder to sing in the choir. So the sisters decide they've got to have some stairs. But they're out of money, after building the whole chapel. What to do? They ponder this.

Then they say a novena to Saint Joseph. For nine days they pray.

About a week later this guy shows up, walking, carrying all his woodworking tools and stuff on the back of a burro. And he builds these stairs using just a hammer and a saw and a couple tubs of water to bend the wood. Not a single nail. No center support. Special double-helix construction—my dad always loved that part. Takes him six months. Then when this mystery carpenter is done, he disappears. Never asks for a cent for his work. Never tells anybody his name. The sisters say it was Saint Joseph himself. But a lot of other people claim that it was their grandpa or somebody in their family, even some guy from Austria.

So anyway, the stairs have been falling apart for years. You can't even get near them now. They're blocked off with that yellow plastic tape like they have at crime scenes.

Esteban clumps over to the stairs, squats down, and looks up. Like he's half expecting somebody to come walking down.

"What's he doing?" Henry whispers.

I shrug. Some minutes go by while we stand there in the doorway, both of us watching Esteban, all three of us watching the staircase.

About a month ago, when Henry and I show up at the homeless shelter, where Sister Celestine forces us to volunteer on Thursday nights, a new man is sitting there with Doris and Dirk, the people who run the place. Some guys show up with a couple trash bags full of stuff. One guy I know hauls an electric toaster around in his trash bag. But this new guy just has a canvas backpack with a bunch of woodworking tools in it. A T-square is sticking out the top. "Meet Esteban," Doris says.

"Hi," we say. He nods.

Doris is reading Esteban the rules of the house. I know them by heart and say them along with her, real soft, for fun. "No guns or weapons. No drinking. No smoking. No over-night guests. If you stay out overnight, you can't come back, because if you don't need the bed, somebody else does. The door is locked at ten o'clock p.m. sharp."

"And ten o'clock doesn't mean 10:01," Dirk chimes in. That's his line. Esteban's nodding, looking serious.

At dinner Esteban keeps his head bent over his plate. If Doris asks him a question, he says, "Yes, ma'am," and "No, ma'am," real polite. Otherwise he doesn't say much. Later, on the porch, he hits Henry up for cigarette money.

The next Thursday, all anybody can talk about is Esteban. Esteban this, Esteban that. "Come out and see the steps Esteban is building for the back porch," Doris says.

So we go look at these steps. They're okay. No work of art, mostly plywood and two-by-sixes.

"Esteban used to be a cabinetmaker," Dirk says. "Take a look at this wall he built in just a couple hours. Now there's a real carpenter!"

"Wow!" says Henry, but he's easily impressed. Me, I've seen better.

"I'm helping him, you know," says one of the other homeless guys, but he's a goofball from New Orleans who says he speaks twenty-seven languages. Nobody pays much attention to him.

"I thought it was our job to give and theirs to receive," says Doris, with a catch in her voice. "But here's this wonderful gift from somebody who has nothing. Nothing at all."

Meanwhile I'm starting to gag at all this oooing and aahing over Esteban. And old Esteban's hammering away on the stairs, acting like he's not hearing this, but I can tell he's eating it up. Henry's smiling proudly. He always thought one of these guys would turn out to be somebody.

"Used to be a cabinetmaker, you know," Henry tells me. "Had his own shop. Like your

Dad used to." As if a hundred people hadn't already told me that.

It's funny what happens next. Everybody starts believing in Esteban. The other homeless guys start doing stuff around the place. One of them puts up a basketball hoop on the garage. The goofball fixes the bike that the shelter keeps for the guys who need it. One of the volunteers asks Esteban to put a new roof on his house for pay. Everybody believes Esteban can make it.

Everyone except me, that is. Personally I don't buy all this good citizen crap. I admit, Esteban cleaned up pretty good. But he's a boozer, just like my old man, and if there's one thing I've learned in life, it's that you can't trust a boozer. But Henry and the others don't have much life experience. So Henry hangs out with Esteban, eating up his stories of hopping trains and great adventures on the road. Esteban even tells Henry he believes in Jesus, couldn't have stuck it out through all this if it wasn't for Jesus. Henry thinks he's making some kind of convert.

"Hey, Leon, maybe we could help him start a business around here," Henry says one night when we're walking home. "He's a cabinetmaker, you know."

"Used to be," I say. *"Used* to be."

"There's something very good about him. Something extraordinary."

"Me," I say, "I don't believe in miracles."

Then Sister Celestine makes me go over extra after school and help Esteban build the new front porch. She figures I should have picked up some carpentry knowledge from my old man.

So when I show the first day, I can see from the corner of the block that Esteban's already out on the front porch working. He looks good when he's working. Smooth. No wasted motion. "Beautiful," my old man used to say when he saw a guy working like that.

So I'm standing around. Esteban goes on working.

"My old man was a carpenter," I say after a while, just because I'm getting bored.

"Yeah?" he says with zero interest, his hands still busy, sure of themselves. Watching a good carpenter at work is like watching a ballet, my old man used to say.

"Maybe he still is," I say. "My old man. A carpenter, I mean."

Esteban goes on hammering. I'm mostly watching, handing him things now and then. Eventually he stops and lights up a cigarette.

"So, Esteban," I say, making conversation, "how'd you end up in a place like this?" Most of these guys like to swap lies about their lives. But Esteban ignores my question. He's just kind of staring at me. "You about eighteen?" he says.

"Yeah."

He nods. Takes a couple draws on his cigarette. "I got a boy must be about your age now. Back in Denver," he says.

About my age. He doesn't even know how old his kid is. For some reason, this sets me off. I almost want to laugh.

"Smart as a whip, that boy of mine," Esteban is saying. "Took after his mama. Learned to read two years before he ever got to school."

"Do me a favor," I say. "Spare me the loving father bullshit. Just tell me straight. How'd a guy like you, who could've made a life for himself, end up a bum?"

Esteban gets a here-we-go-again look in his eyes. He sighs. He taps his right foot for a while. Then looks at me like he's going to start talking.

"No, wait," I say. "You don't have to tell me. I can guess. Let's see, you had it rough when you were a kid—your old man took a strap to you, beat you up, or abused you or something. Or your wife ran around on you. Or maybe . . . maybe it was just too much work for a fun-loving guy like you raising a kid."

Esteban takes a couple more draws on his cigarette, squints at me through the smoke, then flicks the butt into the dirt. "Nope, kid. That ain't it."

I'm all ears, waiting for the big revelation.

"It's simpler than that," he says, his black eyes looking straight at me. "I'm a pure coward."

I snort. "Is that it?" Damn right you're a coward, I want to say. I knew a guy just like you, I want to say.

"I can do this," he says, pointing at the porch and the stairs. He's still looking at me, like he's waiting for me to get it. Then he says, "It's all I got."

And I'm looking at him, still mad, but now I'm seeing a tired-out, beat-up, worn-down, sorry-looking old man. I sit down on the stairs, and I sit like that for a long time.

Finally Esteban says, "I was just wondering, kid, if you was planning to pick up a hammer today, or just sit there moaning?"

I pick up a hammer.

After that I came back each night for almost a week. I got used to Esteban waiting on the steps for me. I got used to the feeling of working, the pounding of our hammers—sometimes to the same beat—and the sound echoing off the other houses. And it was something, that porch we made.

Then Esteban gets his first paycheck from the roofing job and doesn't come back to the house. Nobody knows where he is. Except me. I have a pretty good idea.

So on Thursday, when Henry and I are standing in the kitchen, mixing up the fat mound of house spaghetti that is our specialty, the goofball comes in. He can hardly wait to tell us that Esteban is sitting in the bar around the corner, staying drunk all the time.

Henry doesn't believe him right off. He sticks up for Esteban. Nearly calls the goofball a liar. And then when he does believe it, he says it doesn't change anything. Me, I believe the goofball. But I yell at him to get lost and what business of his is it anyway.

Doris believes him, too. She asks me and Henry to change the sheets on Esteban's bed, soon as we've finished the spaghetti, so that she can give his room to a new guy from San Antonio.

Henry still comes around to the shelter on Thursdays. Me, I don't care what Sister Celestine says. I pretty much go back to hanging with my friends in the market square after school.

So now Esteban is back, outlined with lightning, like God's signpost or something. And the three of us are hanging around the

miraculous staircase, that old spiral of black
and gold wood, like two giant cobras
charmed right off the ground and up to the
choir loft. Waiting.

Then Esteban does a very unmiraculous
thing. Anti-miraculous. He sneaks a swig from
the bottle in his pocket. I snort. This is turning out like I thought it would. But from the
look on Henry's face, Esteban might as well
have punched him in the stomach. I guess
Henry thought Esteban was here to say a
couple Our Fathers. "Maybe you better not
watch this," I say. I cover Henry's eyes from
behind, thinking this will cheer him up. But
Henry knocks my hand away.

Esteban unzips his backpack and gets out
his measuring tape, hammer, level, plumb
bob. Sticks a few shims in the back pocket of
his jeans. Then he walks over and rips away
the yellow crime scene tape at the bottom of
the stairs.

"Uh-oh. Here we go," I say.

The tourist recording has started up again.
"Welcome to the Loretto Chapel." The nuns
are crooning away in Latin.

Esteban doesn't climb the stairs right away.
He runs his gnarly, busted-up old hands
along the part underneath the stairs that's
filled in with plaster painted to look like
wood so the tourists would quit chipping
away miraculous chunks to take home with

them. He runs his hands along the side of the dark curled railing. He circles the staircase, feeling the fine joints, measuring, checking for levelness.

Then he starts climbing. And he's steady as he climbs. He looks like a workman, not a drunk. Better than that. He looks like the young man, the artist, the cabinetmaker come back to life. His hands and his body remember things his mind has forgotten. He looks as graceful as a tightrope walker, as graceful as my old man did when he worked up high.

"Look at that!" says Henry.

"Yeah," I say. "I know."

But those 120-year-old steps creak and moan under his weight, and I'm getting a familiar sick feeling in my stomach.

"What's he doing?" Henry says.

"Getting himself arrested," I say.

"Hey!" yells the girl at the desk. "Hey, hey, HEY!" Her high heels are click-click-clicking across the marble floor. "What do you think you're doing?"

Esteban doesn't answer. He is going about his work, graceful, quick now. Measuring, making ready.

The girl is standing at the bottom of the stairs, her hands on her hips, tapping her foot. "Get down off there, you old bum, or I'm gonna call 911."

It's like she's said the magic words to break the spell. Esteban is an old, dirty bum again. He loses his balance and slips down a step, falling against a rail that creaks ferociously.

Henry looks like he's going to start bawling. That's when I start climbing the miraculous staircase. "Easy, buddy," I say, climbing up beside Esteban with the stairs creaking and groaning and cracking like the very devil.

"Hey, it's the kid. What are you doing here?" Esteban asks in a boozy voice. "I'm gonna fix these stairs for these folks."

"No you are NOT, mister!" says the girl from down below.

"I could use some good help, kid." Esteban's words are slurred together.

"Maybe tomorrow," I say, working my arm under Esteban's shoulder. I start steadying him down the stairs, but I'm thinking that the whole thing is going to collapse any second. So I keep talking. "You can't fix them right now, man. This place is closing."

"Yeah?" He looks surprised.

"Yeah."

Esteban lets me help him over into the entryway. The girl holds the door open and gets out her keys to lock it after us.

"You!" she says, pointing at Esteban. "Stay away from here! You kids, too. Everybody out."

And then we are on the street, in the dark. Esteban stumbles off down the block without a word, and we watch him go.

"You got anything else funny to say about El Milagro?" Henry says to me, real fierce.

I don't answer right away, because I'm smelling Esteban's smell on my hands and my shirt, I'm thinking how I'm not going to be any good with him gone. And I'm thinking of how to tell Henry something important. My old man used to say that a person's got to live in the real world. "Seeing is believing," he'd say. But this is what I want to tell Henry: I'm starting to think my old man got it wrong. I'm starting to see how it could be the other way around.

"No," I say. "No, I don't."

The Owl in the Road

by Stephanie Weller Hanson

It's past ten on a cool June night when I get out of my class in Eden Prairie, Minnesota. I have a forty-five-minute drive across Minneapolis to my home in Saint Paul. My mind is on tonight's class and whether Ben, my sick four-year-old, will sleep tonight. Anderson Lakes Parkway is narrow and isolated, part of it a dark causeway between two lakes. People always drive too fast there.

What was that? Was that an owl in the road?

I peer in my rearview mirror; something's there. I turn around and drive back. The owl is on its feet, unmoving, in the middle of the yellow stripe. I pull my car over to the water's edge and watch two cars pass each other with the owl in the middle. Will the owl fly? It has to fly, I think. I hold my breath and watch its feathers lift in the wind, but it doesn't move.

Clearly the owl's been hit. The Raptor Center at the university is five minutes from my house; they care for injured birds. I could—

could I?—wrap up the owl and carry it there. Is this idea crazy?

I pray hard, then get out of the car. The road is empty and dark. There's a fresh, water-laden breeze from the lake. I hear frogs and crickets, the wind in the high trees. I'm six feet from the owl, then three. It's mottled gray and brown, with vague stripes in front, and it's holding one wing wrong. One lid is down, but the other dark eye watches me. Slowly, it winks.

I stand over the owl, pray again, and let out a sigh. No heavenly insights tonight, it seems. Then, in my mind's eye, I see my Uncle Emmett. Uncle Emmett, who knew horses, dogs, and the farms around Galena, Ohio. When I was a baby, he let me teethe on empty beer bottles while everybody went to church on Sunday. Uncle Emmett never got over Aunt Charlotte's early death from a rheumatic heart. Big, tough-talking, and rotund, but a mush pot at heart. I think of him when I'm in trouble.

"Sheila, darlin'," he says in my mind, "tell me you're not takin' this critter for a ride."

"I'm only thinking about it," I say.

"You're goin' to drive across Minneapolis with a wild bird in back? Goin' sixty miles an hour with the semis leanin' on their horns? What if it goes for you? You could get killed."

"But it's alive, Emmett. And it won't last fifteen minutes in the road."

"You could take it into the woods and leave it," he responds. "At least that way it wouldn't be roadkill."

"But it would still be dead," I answer.

All this time, the owl is standing there with the wind lifting its feathers, like a solitary ghost from an older, wilder world, one without houses and city lights and speeding cars. The owl and the crickets and the wind in the trees are part of that green world—and so am I. Only the metal machine that hit the owl isn't. I get a towel out of the trunk.

Behind me, Emmett says, "I can see the story in the paper tomorra: 'Woman found dead on the freeway with her eyes pecked out. The bird knew enough to fly the coop.' Heh, heh." (Emmett always did enjoy his own jokes.)

I open the back door and start toward the owl, then halt at a sound above me. A span of wings appears, ghostlike, for a moment in the oak tree.

"Must be the mate," I say.

In a low voice, Emmett answers, "Pore critter knows something's wrong, but it can't do one blasted thing to help. I remember."

I hesitate, then drape the towel over the owl's shoulders. It doesn't react. All of a sudden, I feel like the giant at the top of the beanstalk, huge and crude and fumbling. Gingerly, I close my hands around the body and pick it up. Twelve inches of bird, and it weighs only this?

As I walk back, my heart is pounding; even in my fingertips I can feel it. Then I stop in mid-step. My fingertips are touching its feathers in front. It is the owl's heart I feel fluttering. Oh, deep amazement.

Almost at the same instant, I realize my fingers are also half an inch from its curved beak. I hold the owl out at arms' length, ready to let go if it bites me.

I halt at the open back door, and helplessness floods over me. How exactly can I make this work? Can the owl hold on in the back seat? Will the jarring hurt it? Experimentally, I lower the owl to the seat. To my surprise, its talons sink into the velour like roots into deep soil. This owl is *planted.*

Horns blaring metal pounding shouts and engine roaring! I shriek! My head hits the roof.

"Stupid idiot get your stupid car off the road woo-hoo!"

Sixteen-year-old jerk! He and his three buddies have an arm out each window, giving me the one-finger salute. A fountain of curses erupts from Uncle Emmett. (He always was the family champion.)

Silence. I breathe deeply. Emmett peers in at the owl.

"Hm, didn't even move," he says. "Must be in shock."

"Just as well," I answer. I turn the key in the ignition and watch the owl. No movement. But I feel a stab of fear as I hit the gas pedal on the entrance ramp. What exactly will I do if it flies at me while I'm driving? Now Uncle Emmett's talking again.

"If you're goin' to try this cockamamy scheme, it's a good thing you got me along, darlin'," he says. "Now, just stay in the right lane and drive slow—No, not that slow! You'll get a car up your tailpipe!—Right, like that. Then if junior here decides to get a little exercise, you can pull off on the shoulder."

"Good idea," I say.

"'Course with your talent for trouble, you'll probably hit a bridge abutment."

"Thanks a lot."

"So tell me," he says, "when did you get all soft on animals? Why, I bet you eat tofu and watch birdies!"

"I hate tofu," I tell him. "But I'll admit I'm a sucker for animals. And you're a fine one to talk, Emmett. What about your German shepherd?"

"Good old Bozo," he says sentimentally. "Bright as a fifteen-watt bulb—but at least *he* was domesticated."

Ten minutes down the road, I begin to breathe easier. Traffic is light, and so far the owl hasn't budged. Maybe this won't be so hard, after all. I look back. The towel looks oddly regal on the owl's shoulders.

"You know," I tell Emmett, "like it's the King of the Owls."

"Hon," he says, "you read *too many books.*"

I'm laughing as we curve around the cloverleaf for 35-W, where everything changes.

A van and a truck bear down on us with a roar. I barely manage to merge. Another truck pulls even with us and the inside of the car is flooded with diesel fumes and noise. With shaking fingers, I roll up the window. With the hackles rising on the back of my neck, I look back. The owl swivels its head, watching me. The towel is slipping off its back.

"What do I do now?" I say, feeling desperate and stupid at the same instant. "Should I sing to it? You know, Music soothes the savage whatever?"

Emmett's quiet for a second. "How 'bout 'Strangers in the Night?' It's nighttime and you're gettin' stranger by the minute."

"Very funny." My mind's blank for a second, then I start singing, "Kum-ba-yah, my Lord, kum-ba-yah."

"I'll be darned," says Emmett after a minute. I look back. The owl's motionless again.

We're nearly to Crosstown Commons, a spaghetti tangle of curves, ramps, and freeways. It makes me nervous in daylight. And now? My mouth goes dry as I remember that there aren't any shoulders there. I grasp the wheel till my fingers hurt and start the swing to the right.

"Hold on, owl, kum-ba-yah," I warble as two semis and a sports car close on me. The sports car cuts to the left around one semi, which blares its horn, then right in front of me.

"Sheesh! What an idiot," I mutter.

"At least he ain't the one playin' chauffeur for an owl," says Emmett.

We make it onto I-94, and the blessed shoulder reappears. We're through the worst of it now. I look back. The towel is on the seat; the owl blinks at me, but I just keep driving.

"Hush, little baby, don't say a word," I sing as we cross the Mississippi. We're nearly home, and suddenly I feel shiningly happy. I pull up in front of the house, and consider taking the owl inside.

Uncle Emmett rouses himself. "Sheila, darlin', don't be a lamebrain! Leave the bird here!"

I race up the stairs to the house. The living room is dark; Ben's asleep. Charlie's just getting into bed.

"Hi. You're late," he says.

"Something happened," I say, then I see what he's thinking. "No! No, I didn't have an accident, but—"

(How exactly am I going to explain this?)

"—I have an owl in the car."

"You what?"

"I have an owl in the car," I repeat.

I have to remind him to put on clothes before he goes out the door. I watch him sprint down to the street and peer in the car window.

(I tell Charlie that he has only one failing as a husband: he just doesn't connect with animals the way I do. I remember what he said so despairingly to his brother after spending Christmas with my family. "They're all intelligent, articulate people. And what do they talk about when they get together once a year? Their dogs and cats and birds.")

Charlie climbs the stairs and stops in front of me. "That's an owl, all right," he says. "And, please, don't even think about bringing it inside."

"I wasn't going to," I lie.

I call the Raptor Center and listen to the recorded message while I thumb through my Peterson's bird guide. Those brown eyes stand out on the page. What I have is a barred owl, and what the vet school has is an animal emergency room to help it.

As I start the car, the owl shifts from one leg to the other. When I brake for a stop sign, I hear a loud FLAP as it rediscovers its wings.

"Run them stop signs, Hon," says Uncle Emmett.

"Right," I say weakly.

The vet follows me to the parking lot with a towel and a glove. I watch her pull the padded leather gauntlet up to her armpit, then she deftly covers the owl's head with the towel.

"Next time you do a rescue," she says (and I hear Uncle Emmett snort), "put the towel over the head. They tend to go to sleep when you do that."

At long last, in the bright glare of the reception room, the owl decides to fly. The vet is holding it by the legs, but it seems to fill the room. It's both terrified and unmistakably fierce. Its wingspan is four feet; its yellow talons are three inches long.

"Holy God," I whisper, staring at it. I decide that Charlie's absolutely right: my family is weird about animals, and I'm the weirdest one of all. I cross the parking lot feeling chastened.

"You know," I tell Uncle Emmett as I drive home, "you're a pretty good stand-in for a guardian angel."

"Listen, darlin'," he says. "You got away with it this time. But don't you *ever* try a damn stupid stunt like that again."

I promise Uncle Emmett that I never will, but I feel exultant. My injured owl might just survive with the help of the Raptor Center. But more than that, I have been part of the magic dark of the woods, in the sweet night air, where wild things fly. I have felt *life* in the beating of an owl's heart. I feel as if I'm a child of six again, and the world is quivering with possibility.

Five months later, I stand with Charlie and Ben on a cloudy day at Highland Park Reserve, two miles east of Anderson Lakes. The Raptor Center is doing its fall release. As we watch, my barred owl, healthy now, is tossed into the air like a basketball. (I wish Uncle Emmett could be here. He'd like that part.) Above us, the owl unfurls its wings and, with slow, powerful wing beats, circles once over the crowd, then heads west toward Anderson Lakes, free again. I squeeze Ben's hand and tell him this is a wonderful day.